YOU'VE TRIED MARRIAGE.
BEFORE YOU TRY REMARRIAGE,
TRY LIVING.

As a formerly married woman you are about to enter a fiercely competitive world—competing for a job, for a man, for an identity. Accept the challenge. Never before in history have women had such an opportunity to build for themselves.

Develop faith in yourself.
Use your time, talent, and energy
to the fullest.
YOU CAN DO WHATEVER
YOU THINK YOU CAN DO!

Other SIGNET Books You'll Want to Read

What Every Formerly Married Woman Should Know

Answers to the Most Intimate
Questions Formerly
Married
Women Ask

by
Louise Montague Athearn

A SIGNET BOOK
NEW AMERICAN LIBRARY
TIMES MIRROR

SIGNET TRADEMARK REG. U.S. PAT. OFF. AND FOREIGN COUNTRIES
REGISTERED TRADEMARK—MARCA REGISTRADA
HECHO EN CHICAGO, U.S.A.

SIGNET, SIGNET CLASSICS, MENTOR,
PLUME and MERIDIAN BOOKS
are published by The New American Library, Inc.,
1301 Avenue of the Americas, New York, New York 10019

FIRST PRINTING, JULY, 1974

1 2 3 4 5 6 7 8 9

PRINTED IN THE UNITED STATES OF AMERICA

Contents

Introduction

As a person who has stepped out of the role of wife by death or divorce, you now face the world as a formerly married woman. All our institutions, living arrangements, social structures are shaking, falling apart and rearranging. The whole condition of women is in a state of flux. New philosophies woo us from all sides as old familiar behavior patterns are being pulled out from under us.

To lament the changes, fear the new philosophies, and hang on to outmoded ideas won't make the world change less. It will only make your adjustment harder. Whether you recognize it as such or not, divorce or death have made you a liberated woman. By "liberated" I mean free to move ahead under your own banner.

As a formerly married woman you are about to enter a fiercely competitive world. You must compete for a job, compete for a man, and compete for an identity. You will also find that you must compete with men as well as women. There is help available to you, but this help is in no way equal to your needs. When I was first divorced and found so very little help, I decided to write a book that would be my effort in helping other divorced women. Based on my experiences, *The Divorcée's Handbook* outlined the problems I faced and offered solutions that worked for me.

However, I barely scratched the surface. After publication of *The Divorcée's Handbook* I began to receive mail from divorced and widowed women all over the country. Each letter contained a particular problem I hadn't mentioned, or one whose solution they felt I had not covered in depth. I corresponded with these women and talked to hundreds more, both in person and on my radio program. I compiled an eight-page questionnaire that I sent to women in every state, in every walk of life.

From that research came this book. These are the most intimate, pressing problems facing the formerly married woman today. My hope is that answers to one woman will help answer the questions of another woman. This form of person-to-person help has survived the ages. The mass information centers can never replace the comforting aid of a friend who listens.

There are, however, no pat answers when it comes to choosing a way of life. This you can only do for yourself. You might ask—"But how do I know what will work for me? It's been years since I was a single woman!" One thing I can assure you; what worked then most certainly cannot be counted upon to work now. Never before in the history of women have we had such opportunity to build for ourselves. Never have we had such choice. To go back to our options of even twenty years ago would be dishonest to ourselves and to our children.

Whatever road or roads you take, you are being propelled into the future at a shocking rate of speed. The only person who will constantly share these roads with you is you. Accept this as your challenge. Develop *faith* in yourself. Identify with good. Use your time, talent, and energy to the absolute fullest. It doesn't matter that you were "formerly married." What does matter is that you are "presently you"—you as never ever before possible.

LOUISE MONTAGUE ATHEARN

Hillsborough, California

When Does the Loneliness Leave?

It doesn't. Loneliness must be treated to be cured. The loneliness that replaces grief and the loneliness of a divorce share the same debilitating characteristics. Although one is an act of nature and one the act of law, the same voids remain.

The only lasting way to treat loneliness is to fill these voids. Your days as a married woman developed a certain pattern. When the familiar routine was disrupted you were left with minutes and hours all your own. The usual reaction is to feel a sense of loss, a sense of loneliness often followed by an overpowering flood of helplessness.

Loneliness can be dangerous because of the things you do to erase the pain and fill the void. Rationally you should sift through the activities and people that fill your days, rejecting some, accepting others, making choices and decisions. If you wallow in loneliness and self-pity you lose your sense of judgment and often turn to temporary solutions that remain as permanent guilts. As a guideline of just *how* to treat loneliness, I offer this chart. Copy it down (altered to fit your particular living pattern) and tape it to the inside of your closet door.

> I. UPON ARISING: Turn on the radio and listen to the news as you dress. The country's problems are far more staggering than yours. You should be aware of what is going on in the outside world. You also become a more interesting person because you *are* aware.
>
> II. WITH COFFEE: Keep a small spiral notebook in your purse. Take it out now and list the things you intend to do today. This list should include phone calls, letters, errands, activities, projects—not just housework or your job. During the day check them off with a red pencil as you do them. Tomorrow morning start a list on the next page beginning with the things you didn't finish today.
>
> III. BEFORE DINNER: This is the time *he* used to come home. Whatever routine the two of you had to-

1

gether—break it. If you have children, this time should now be devoted *entirely* to them. Ask to see their homework. Let them help with dinner. *Listen* to their problems.

If you don't have children this should be your pamper time. Take a bubble bath, polish your toenails, give yourself a facial. Be as totally hedonistic as you like. Fix yourself a decent dinner and sit down to eat it. A woman living alone often does not eat properly and her health, looks, and vitality suffer as a result.

IV. AFTER DINNER: This is *take stock time*. In another notebook begin a list of things you would like to do. A good place to start is with your job situation. If you didn't work while married, now is the time to start deciding what you want to do—because you *must* do something. Make a list of ideal jobs and under each put the requirements to obtain that job. Start making some rational decisions about your future.

If you already have a job, begin thinking about your future in that job. What is the next step? What additional training do you need? How do you go about obtaining that training? Just seeing these things written down is an enormous step forward. Begin to investigate the classes you can take at night school. Why should your evenings be determined by a man? If you have children, arrange for a baby-sitter two nights a week and stick to it!

V. WEEK ENDS: If you have children, plan some family outing, even if it's just a trip to the park or the museum. Get some maps and books from the library and look up places of interest and historical value. Involve the children in the planning and let them make suggestions. Start now to plan for vacation. Half the fun is the preparation.

If you don't have children—go anyway. Or call a married friend and take her children. It will be a treat for you both. But don't hesitate to go alone to an art show or the theater. You'll be amazed at how much fun *you* are.

VI. ENTERTAIN: Once a month, preferably twice or even three times, invite dinner guests. Choose from your family, your married friends, your associates at work. Don't always think in terms of even numbers. If you have a single male friend you would like to ask, fine. If not, fine. It's *your* dinner party! Spend some time

2

reading a recipe book and prepare something new. Bake a truly gooey and delicious dessert. It doesn't have to be an expensive dinner. You can become famous for a great spaghetti.

TO BE AVOIDED: Loneliness provokes the same reactions in enough women to be predictable. In order not to fall into these harmful patterns, avoid the following:

1. *Liquor:*

If your pattern was to have a cocktail or two with your husband before dinner, it's likely that you will miss the drinks as much (or more) than you miss him. There is nothing wrong with mixing yourself a drink to sip while you prepare dinner. But, watch it. There are an alarming number of women in this country who are silent sippers. You don't have to be falling-down-drunk to be considered an alcoholic.

I am right now watching two very attractive single women become alcoholics. How do I know this is happening? Because their excessive drinking is beginning to show in their physical, creative, and emotional lives. Let me describe what has and is happening to Beverly.

When Beverly was divorced three years ago, she received the family home, custody of the two children, and $650.00 a month. Since she and her former husband had lived in the house for fifteen years the payments were down to $178.00 a month. By carefully managing she found she was able to live in the home and take care of her children without taking a job. Her children at that time were fourteen and sixteen.

I strongly suggested to Beverly that she should take a job after her divorce even if she could live quite nicely on her child support and alimony. She laughed and said she didn't know how to do anything and she thought it would be fun to just be a single woman. And she did have fun. She had a great many dates, always seemed to be rushing home from a lunch date to dress for a dinner date.

As I said, this was three years ago. Today Beverly has the tiny red lines beginning to show under her skin, just under her eyes and around her nose. Although her arms and legs are slim she has a decided "pot" for a stomach. Her day begins with orange juice and vodka, a Bloody Mary or two or three for lunch and then, well, it's time to start the cocktail hour.

3

Three Martinis before dinner, a glass or two of wine, then why not an after-dinner drink? A nightcap before bed and Beverly firmly says to me, "Louise, I am *not* an alcoholic." What do you say?

Physically she is losing her looks, her body, her health. Creatively she has absolutely no ambition to do anything. Her son, now nineteen and a freshman in college, has urged her to go back to school. No, that is too much work. I found her a part-time job in a tennis shop. No, she couldn't accept it, she has given up her interest in tennis. Her major endeavor is to keep going, keep drinking.

Emotionally she is not able to sustain a relationship. A man she cared deeply about told me he didn't want the responsibility of trying to re-interest her in real life. She now lives in the foggy world of the walking-around-alcoholic. Any effort he made to make her look squarely at herself ended in tears and pleadings.

Beverly is physically, creatively, and emotionally affected by the bottle. She has robbed herself of a real life. She is disaster-bound and for absolutely no valid reason. A woman with everything to live for, she has gone out of her way to pick the path of no reward.

Janette is the second woman I know personally whom I would say was dominated by liquor. A widow with a very substantial income, a lovely home, and a nice group of friends, you would imagine her in a quite enviable position. Not so. Instead of continuing to see her friends, enjoy her home, or travel, Janette has become a complete recluse. Her beautiful home, even with the dedicated help of a housekeeper, is always a shambles. Meals are never organized or served on time. Her oldest son is married and her younger son in college. They seldom come home.

At any hour of the day you can find Janette with a teacup of "sippin' whiskey" in her hand. Her claim is, "I don't drink. I just sip a bit to boost my morale." This claim may fool Janette, but it certainly fools no one else. Her housekeeper has told me she "sips" at least a bottle a day, and sometimes more.

Her second main pleasure in life is reading and on warm days she sips and reads by the pool. On cold days she sips and reads by the fire or in her big four-poster bed with its incredible pile of tiny silk pillows.

Her constant companions are four to six Lhasa Apsos. I am never sure of the number, but I know they are a legion. Totally as spoiled and indulged as their mistress, no room is off limits to them, no furniture forbidden their company, no rug unfamiliar with their toilet habits. The whole scene is Tennessee Williams. Janette's once fine mind is becoming pickled. Her health is suffering and her friends have all but abandoned her. I have tried to jar her loose from this prison but she is unmovable. This is the way she wants to live. When I think of all she could do with her money, the exciting life she could lead, the contributions she could make, I am almost sick. It's a waste of her life, talent, and resources. Although she must have psychological problems, drinking is certainly no answer.

2. *Bars:*

Single women go to bars more for the noise and activity than to have a drink. The "happiness" you experience resting on a barstool is temporary and hollow. The people you meet are all too frequently problem-ridden and unreal. When you leave the bar your loneliness will return a thousand times more acute. You will have coupled it with guilt and a feeling of worthlessness.

3. *Overeating:*

Turning to food is another opiate for a feeling of loneliness. When you think no one cares it's so easy to walk into the kitchen (or a candy store) and reach for something that tastes good. If this pattern is allowed to continue you will find unattractive extra pounds added to your other problems. So each time you start to eat something, say to yourself: "Who *am* I eating for— the real me who needs a certain amount of good food, or the *un*real me who is working at cross purposes to myself and is just after temporary relief, no matter what the price?"

4. *TV:*

Indiscriminate television watching is an addiction as serious as drugs. The effects are similar. You are "frozen" in front of the set and your growth as a person is stunted. You rely on the noise and the movement to dull your senses and keep you from thinking. You become a shut-in rather than an active mingler in society.

5

Married women watch a great deal of television. If you were one of those married ladies who had morning coffee with the news, made beds to a game show, and spent the afternoon ironing to an old movie—break the pattern! Illustrating the theory of Parkinson who says we stretch the task to fill the hours, the woman who works to TV is working to about one-tenth of her potential. TV should play a small part in the active life of an unmarried woman. You should be too busy living life to watch it being fictionalized. Nothing is more exciting than your own accomplishments!

5. *Telephone:*

Used to communicate, it's a fine invention. Used as a means for killing time, it's a menace. Have a valid purpose in mind before you pick up the receiver. And don't call the man you date "just to chat." Men are far more realistic about the phone and use it to better advantage. When tempted to call him say to yourself, "If he wanted to talk to me he knows where I am." Then go do something constructive and don't think about the phone at all.

VII. TO BE PREPARED: When faced with a situation your husband used to handle, you often feel a sense of loneliness—or aloneness. Actually, this is a feeling of helplessness. To avoid these moments, use one of your evenings to make a master list of phone numbers entitled "IF I CAN'T DO IT, HERE IS SOMEONE WHO CAN." Use the classified section of the phone book as a source. Or call friends and ask who they use. But *find* someone in each of the following categories. Make up a list and put it in a looseleaf notebook in the following fashion.

Bicycle Repair Shop   _____
Children's School   _____
Church   _____
Dentist   _____
Doctor (or Doctors)   _____
Electrician   _____
Emergency Road Service   _____
Firemen (local)   _____
Garage Mechanic   _____
Gas Company   _____

Insurance Man	_____
Lawnmower Repair Shop	_____
Lawyer	_____
Locksmith	_____
Policemen (local)	_____
Plumber	_____
Rescue Service	_____
Tax Man	_____
Telephone Company	_____
Veterinarian	_____
Water Department	_____

Now, when you get a flat tire, or the toilet overflows, or your income tax form arrives, or you're locked out of your house—you'll know what to do! And without calling *him* . . . or flopping down in a chair to feel sorry for yourself.

All this super planning and organizing may not overcome all the loneliness. But everything suggested here *works*—and to your advantage! Frantically trying to fill your life with pointless activity works to your *dis*advantage. The sooner you take over your life, the greater are your chances for success—in everything!

QUESTION TWO

Where Are the Best Places to Meet Men?

No matter how full your life is with a good constructive job, taking care of a home or apartment, rearing children or raising animals, most women, in their hearts, long for a good man. And quite honestly most women would prefer to be married. Therefore, the most frequently asked question is: Where and how do I meet eligible men?

HERE IS WHAT MY RESEARCH SHOWS:

1. *Through your married friends*
   Not only is this the nicest way to meet single men, but if remarriage is your goal, it has the highest statistics

7

of success. Married couples are the first to know who in the neighborhood, office, or plant is available. Married women know what's happening because this type of news is a big part of their lives. (You remember how much time you spent "chatting" when you were married?) So be quite candid with your married friends and remind them, from time to time, to keep you in mind when a single man appears in their lives.

Keep in mind, also, that friendship is a two-way street. When a friend calls and invites you to dinner to meet someone, offer to take her children during the day or to bring dessert, or both. Let her know you appreciate what she is doing for you.

2. *On the job*

I can't stress how important it is for you to work at a job. If you have small children and simply can't have a full-time job, take a part-time one. If your support money or income from your husband's estate is such that you don't need to work, take on a volunteer job. But be sure the volunteer job is not exclusively in a back room addressing envelopes. Become a museum guide or work on a civic project that has male members.

Getting a job, as I said in question one, is just the first step. From the vantage point of being out in the commercial world you can look around at what else is available and start your list of how to go about getting a better job. While you are doing this, be alert. The commercial world is full of men.

3. *Pursuing an interest*

When your life begins to be more organized you should make time to pursue your hobby or interest. If you have no special interest, start thinking of what you have always thought you would like to do. If tennis appeals to you, find out through your Park Department where lessons are offered. If you have strong political persuasions, work for the candidate of your choice. If you have always wanted to speak Spanish, look into a night school class through an adult education department. I wouldn't suggest a needlework class as a place to meet men. You can check out a book and learn that at home. Make your hours spent away from home count for something, especially if these hours involve leaving your children

8

with a sitter. The more you learn the more interesting you become.

4. *Traveling*

Although this is a most pleasurable way to meet men, it does take time and money. This doesn't mean you can't travel at some future date. You can begin, now, to carefully plan a trip for some *specific time* in the future. If you have always dreamed of seeing the Greek Islands, find out exactly how much it would cost for you to go. Then start a systematic saving plan that will get you there! Explore the possibility of joining a charter group. Check out some books on Greek culture. You might even take Greek lessons at night school. All these things will add significant meaning to your trip, even if you don't meet someone at the Parthenon.

Don't be frightened by the prospect of traveling alone. It's great fun! Your fears are an indication of a lack of confidence in yourself. Plan your first trip as a short junket. This will give you the confidence and desire to plan more travel. The key word here is "plan." Knowing exactly where you are going, how you are going to get there, what you are going to do once there—all this planning removes a great deal of apprehension and makes for a far better experience.

The experience of travel is very educational and widens your interests. This makes you attractive to men wherever you meet them. Many, many men travel alone. There is no reason that women can't do this also. Why not enjoy the thrill of actually planning an adventure on your own, saving the money for it, and making it all come true. Start by examining road maps of your state. Then look up other states, Canada and Mexico. Soon you'll graduate to the atlas and that's *guaranteed* to stir your travel urge.

5. *With your children*

If you have children, you know how many school and after-school activities request parental attendance. These functions are a splendid way to meet unmarried men. High on the list are PTA night meetings, open house, Cub Scouts, and Little League. Divorced men with children often make it a point not to miss any of their children's programs. Ask your children. They always seem to know which are the divorced or widowed parents.

9

Plan to participate in sports with your children. It's good for them and great for you. If you don't swim, play tennis, skate, ski, ride, bicycle, or sail, at least take them for a long walk. Children have no problem meeting people and you never know with whom they'll strike up a conversation.

If your children are high school or college age, encourage them to be alert for interesting single men. A friend of mine who teaches at our local Junior College says he has met some of his most interesting dates through his students. He is now seeing the mother of a boy he taught three years ago. When the boy's mother got her divorce, the son called my friend and asked him over to dinner. The boy said he knew both of them well and thought they would enjoy each other. They do.

Surely I am not suggesting you make procurers of your children. To be continually harping on the subject of available men would soon disgust them. They do know your situation, and a casual remark should be all that's necessary. Introducing you to a single man may never have occurred to them. Children are like that, you know.

One of my mother's widowed friends married the father of her daughter's husband. The father lived in Eastern Canada and had never been to California. When the first grandchild was born the father insisted that his father fly out to visit. After meeting the new grandmother, the new grandfather extended his visit an extra two weeks.

On returning to Canada he called her regularly and wrote nany letters. A month later he sent my mother's friend a plane ticket to come to visit him, which she hesitated to accept. My mother urged her to go, went into her bedroom and actually packed her suitcase. Her daughter and son-in-law drove her to the airport.

That was five years ago and she is still in Canada, very happily married and living a totally new life. She has written my mother a dozen times to thank her for pulling the suitcase down from the closet. She said she needed that first physical act to send her out into a new world. The son maintains he knew all along they were perfect for each other, and that was why he insisted on the first visit.

As An Added Help, Here Are the Ways Not to Meet Men:

1. *In bars*

   (*See* Question One.) Of course you can meet men in bars. But again, if you are looking for a meaningful relationship, not just a night of fun and games, your chances of finding such a man in a bar are slim. That goes for all kinds of bars, from the neighborhood saloon to the large anonymous cocktail lounges.

   Some large cities have singles' bars that cater to the unmarried as an after-work meeting place. Frequently such places are a waste of precious time that can be better spent pursuing your goals and interests. When you sit at a corner table, nonchalantly fingering the ash tray, you aren't fooling anyone but yourself. You might as well put a sign around your neck that says, "I'm lonesome, available, and not particular."

2. *In resort atmospheres*

   Going to the mountains to ski or to the beach to sit in the sun is great fun, good exercise, and a nice change of pace. But heading for these areas with the specific purpose of meeting someone can be a big disappointment. Resorts are not inexpensive, so make it quite clear to yourself why you are going before you put out all that money.

   If you decide to go to a resort, do what you came to do. If it was to ski, then ski. You'll stand a far better chance of meeting someone queued up at the tow line than hanging around the lodge. It takes a great deal of time and money to be a "playgirl." The gossip columns and glossy magazine articles seldom tell the whole truth. If you are longing to be in such a crowd lazing around a pool, sailing the Caribbean, or hopping a jet to Mexico, keep in mind that such a life is a full-time job and definitely not for amateurs.

   Even if your way is paid in this kind of living, you earn every penny of it. The playgirl works twenty-four hours a day and her position is in constant jeopardy. Youth and stamina are a must and it's difficult to look your best when you are staying up all night, drinking too much, worrying about where you'll be next week.

   Living in southern California in the midst of the entertainment industry, I observed many beautiful girls trying desperately to make the big time partying circuit. Their pattern was predictable; be around the big parties, be at the beach clubs, be aboard the biggest yachts, be there, be available, keep going, keep trying. If you ask them truthfully what they are after, the honest ones admit they want to marry a wealthy man.

As I said, I've seen many such girls. Some were extremely good at what they did. Some were not only very clever but totally ingenious in their ability to be what they wanted to be—playthings for playboys. I don't know why this life still attracts the numbers of players it does, because the odds are not favorable. Of all the playgirls I've observed, I only know one who actually landed her big rich fish. Playgirls seem to get playboys—not real men.

3. *Singles' clubs and "date bureaus"*

There have been a great many groups started on the premise of help for divorced people. I'm sure these groups have done some good. But I certainly wouldn't join one strictly to meet men. Every woman who joins is single. Why put yourself in such competition? It can't help but bring out the worst in most women. The men will hardly be looking for a meaningful relationship when they have such a potpourri from which to choose. Spend your time where it will have the greatest return for you.

Another supposed "help" that falls into this category is the "date bureau" or computerized mate-finding. What these people purport to do is to put you in contact with men who share your likes, hobbies, interests, politics, morals, religion, and hopes for the world. You pay an entrance fee and they give you a vast form to fill out. This form is fed into the computer and the answers "matched" to those of the men. Ideally an athletic blue-eyed man who bowls, shoots, votes Republican, doesn't go to church but wants a nice girl, will be "matched" with a dark-haired athletic girl who bowls, votes Republican, has nothing against nonreligious men, and is a very nice girl. Notice I said ideally.

My four teen-agers decided this would be just the thing for me so they answered an ad in the paper, paid the fee, and brought home a three-page multiple choice form to fill out. Thrilled that they would uncover a whole new world for me, the five of us poured over the form. But our joy was short lived. After name, address, and phone number came the lines:

"I Have No Children"   ☐
"I Have One Child"   ☐
"I Have Two Children"   ☐
"I Have Three Children"   ☐
"I Have More Than Three Children"   ☐

I had to "X" that last box. Then came the question about how you class yourself.

"I Am Considered Beautiful"   ☐
"I Am Considered Nice-Looking"   ☐
"I Am Considered Average-Looking"   ☐
"I Am Below Average-Looking"   ☐

My youngest child reached for the pencil and put a big black "X" after beautiful. "After that last question, Mom, it's the only thing that will help." Obviously his serious remark struck us as terribly funny and we all laughed til our sides ached. Then we had a marvelous time imagining what type of man would request a divorced woman with salt and pepper hair, four children, a dog, three cats, who taught Sunday school, liked to water ski, play tennis, read in bed, was a good cook, but who yawned at 9 P.M. Computers, we decided, were not for us. We voted to keep free-lancing.

Paying money to be put into contact with someone is about as desperate a measure as I can imagine. You are a worthwhile person, one with goals and interests, and you will meet men in your daily life. Don't be misled by those who operate a business and make money on loneliness.

Whenever you have to "pay" for companionship (i.e., dancing clubs) you are a sitting duck for "opportunists." You don't have to be wealthy to attract the parasite who lives on lonely women. When you have to pay to go to parties, pay to take lessons, pay to dance, you are literally twirling the dollars away.

I heard of a widow in her sixties who put a second mortgage on her home to buy a "life membership" in a dancing group. And this was just the beginning. She then paid for extra lessons, bought the different costumes, and went into "competition," all of which cost a great deal more money. When it seemed that she might lose her home, her son stepped in and with the help of the family lawyer, demanded the return of her money. The son attended one of the dances and said it was a pitiful sight. All the women "students" were his mother's age or older. All the young men teachers were cynical, and laughed at the women behind their backs.

Some dancing schools can be as unfortunate for lonely older men as they are for women. For example, the young woman teacher who makes them pay heavily for the thrill of putting their arms around her waist. The whole concept of paying for fun and companionship is degrading and debilitating. It literally robs you of self-respect and lessens your chances of finding true happiness.

Conclusion:

The best way to meet men is to live your life with purpose and direction. Men will come into your life in any number of ways—through your job, your friends, your interests, your children, your family, your church, your hobbies. The key word in all of the above is *your*. It is *your* life and *your* right to be happy. No true lasting happiness is based on money, good times, false fun. You don't buy men and you don't buy happiness.

QUESTION THREE

Should I Move and Start a New Life?

A very tempting answer to *any* problem is to ignore it or run away from it. Just to move with the idea that your problems and your loneliness are going to remain in the town you left, is a false notion. Everything you feel, worry about, or long for, is locked in your head. Rationally you can only *think* it away.

However, there are certainly times when a move *is* a good thing. But the move must be a move *toward* something, not away from it. The advantages must outweigh the disadvantages. To help you make the decision, here are lists of things to consider.

1. Your home where you now live
2. Your family in the area
3. Your job
4. Your friends
5. Your familiar routines
6. Your ability to get around the town or city
7. Your community identity
8. Your church
9. Your lawyer and legal help
10. Your medical and dental help
11. Your local merchants and service people

Read carefully through the list. Then, after each item, describe how it specifically applies to you. For instance:

Item 1: *Your Home or Apartment:* Write down what it costs you. Then describe the neighborhood, accessibility to work, resale value, whatever you think is important about it.

Item 2. *Your Family:* List who they are and how often you see them. Consider how much of a part they play in your life.

Item 3. *Your Job:* Consider what type of job it is, the pay, hours, interest, anything that describes it. Remember if it was a hard job to get and what it means to you.

Item 4. *Your Friends:* Do you have trouble meeting people? Are your current friends important in your social life? Will their friendship and group activity be missed?

Item 5. *Your Routine:* Because you are known in the area in which you now live, you have a familiar pattern. You know how to anticipate happenings and plan for them. You know approximately what each day will bring. Outline a typical week in your life and see how it reads.

Item 6. *Your Ability to Get Around:* When you live in one area you learn the transportation systems, know the short cuts, feel secure in directions. This is all part of your identity. Do you locate easily?

Item 7. *Your Community Identity:* Living in a certain area you participate in activities, help collect for charitable causes, support the candidate of your choice. This identity is built gradually as you build your reputation among the people of the community. List what you do and what it means to you.

Item 8. *Your Church:* Perhaps you teach Sunday School, serve on a committee or sing in the choir. List these things. See what part of your life they fill.

Item 9. *Your Lawyer and Legal Help:* The lawyer who handled your divorce or probate knows all about your case. If there are some parts of it that still need attention, consider this. Perhaps you have family money or business matters that are now handled by a lawyer. Will your leaving be a hindrance in his conducting these affairs? Go over all these possibilities.

Item 10. *Doctors and Dentists:* An important association in life is to feel your doctor and your dentist *know* you and you in turn have faith in them. Put down the names of the medical people important in your life.

Item 11. *Local Merchants and Service People:* This means all the people you buy from or deal with—market, shoe repair, plumber, insurance agent, TV repairman—anyone you have faith in. Check your phone list and put down all the familiar reliable names.

When you have finished the list go back over it and read your answers. This is your life as you now know it. Be sure you have looked objectively at all the pluses and minuses. Don't gloss over things in an attempt to hurry a move. Don't dwell on trivial inconveniences to discourage a move. Once you feel you have been honest with yourself, go on to the next list, which outlines the things you hope to gain.

WHAT YOU HOPE TO GAIN BY MOVING

1. A better place to live
2. Distance from your family
3. Greater career opportunity
4. New friends and expanded social life
5. A new identity
6. An area with more to offer
7. A chance for more community involvement
8. A new church
9. Additional legal aid
10. Expanded medical or dental aid
11. More diversified shopping

Item 1. *The New Place You Will Be Living In:* If you don't know too much about the area, write to the Chamber of Commerce. Get an issue of the local paper and see what the housing situation is. Make a trip to the area and look at the places to rent. It would not be a good idea to consider buying until you've lived there awhile.

Item 2. *Leaving Your Family:* At some time we all feel stifled by our family and would like to be more on our own. This feeling, however, is not reason enough to warrant a move. Be honest. Now is the time to make all the consider-

16

ations. One consideration would be the cost of transportation to see your family.

Item 3. *Greater Career Opportunities:* A move should definitely benefit you in this area. Again, visit the new place, read the want ads, contact an employment agency. If you have a profession such as nursing or teaching, write to the hospitals and school board to see exactly what is available and the salary offered.

Item 4. *New Friends and Social Life:* If you feel you would like to meet new people, a move is a plus. But consider how you are going to do it. Do you have friends in the new area who can help you get started? You can also get a fairly accurate description of social life from the local paper. Find another single woman in the area and ask her opinion of the social life.

Item 5. *A New Identity:* It is a glamorous idea to think about starting a new life. You do learn as you live and there are undoubtedly mistakes you would like to forget. But you don't want to be so anonymous that you cease to exist. That's one of the drawbacks to moving to a very large city. It will take awhile to acquire a new identity.

Item 6. *An Area with More to Offer:* If your present community is limited in educational, creative, artistic outlets, a move to an area with more to offer may be a good thing. Again, check out the new area. Rents in town may be so high you have to live in the suburbs. This would add transportation costs to your new activities. All research you do will be enormously valuable in making your final decision.

Item 7. *A Chance for More Community Involvement:* Your situation may be such that you have extra free time on your hands and would like a major volunteer job and community involvement. This is to be applauded and encouraged. You should be in an area where your services are needed. Have the commitment before you uproot your household.

Item 8. *A New Church:* Perhaps religion plays no major part in your life. In this case a church affiliation is not important. But if it is, joining a church in a new community is a very good way to get acquainted. Letters from the leader of your present affiliation would be most helpful in smoothing the way into a new group.

Item 9. *Additional Legal Aid:* You may be facing a difficult trial or child custody battle and desire expanded legal consultants. If you have no pressing legal matters, this item should not weigh heavily in your decision, one way or the other.

Item 10. *Expanded Medical or Dental Aid:* You may have

need of medical aid not available in your present small town. That would be a plus for moving. But if you're considering the move to have a face lift or some other onetime operation, it's better to go do it and return to your own area. Be honest.

Item 11. *More Diversified Shopping:* This could hardly be a determining factor in the move unless you live so far out in the country shopping is a problem. The important thing is to consider all effects of the move.

After you have looked at all the pros and cons of moving you should have an accurate picture of what the move will do to, or *for* you. Now, if you have children, go over the list with *them* in mind. Give careful consideration to their friends, families, schools, dentists. They may not like the thought of a new life at all. They may have some definite ideas that hadn't occurred to you and they must certainly be considered.

Let me tell you how moving affected three formerly married women. The first woman I have never met in person. She was forty-three at the time of her husband's death, and went back to her profession, nursing. After a year she felt she was not really needed in the small hospital in the town where she lived. She wrote to me and said she wanted to go back to school and become a lab technician, but there were no facilities in her area. She had two children who were happy in their schools, she lived in a nice area, and her friends were important to her life. Her question to me was whether she should move to a certain large city.

I recommended that she visit the new large city and check many of the same things just listed. I suggested that she start first with the hospitals and see if she could get a job. A week later I got an enthusiastic letter from her saying that on her first interview at the largest hospital in the area she was hired on the spot and even started her orientation in street clothes! She had decided then and there to move and her children were not too upset with the idea when she told them what had happened.

When I last heard from her she had given up the idea of becoming a lab technician. She had become head operating-room nurse and felt totally needed and appreciated. Her move was a complete success. She and her children were very happy.

The second woman I met while I was on a publicity tour in a southern state. She was the hostess on a morning TV interview show. As we had coffee and a get-acquainted interview before the show, she confided to me that she had been a divorcée but that I was *not* to mention it on the air. I asked why and she said her audience thinks of her as a happily married woman and this was the image she wanted. I was a bit befuddled by this. I couldn't imagine what harm would be done if her audience knew she had at one time been divorced.

After the show she thanked me for the interview and for keeping the secret. She said she had moved to this city after her divorce to start her life over and she didn't want *anything* to go wrong. She said she had changed her name, her hair color, and had lost fifteen pounds. Her new husband (of three years) was a widower when he met her and I judged by her conversation that he was ten to twelve years her senior. I asked his occupation and she said he was a city official and planning to run for mayor.

The third woman I like to call "The Old-Lady-in-the-Vinegar-Bottle." Remember the fairy tale of the woman who lived in the vinegar bottle and was utterly discontent? She wished and wished for something better. Finally she woke up in a cottage, then a mansion, then a castle, then a kingdom. But each time she was still discontent. To end the story, the Magic Fairy puts the whining lady back in the same vinegar bottle!

My friend, however, is the vinegar-bottle lady in reverse. She had a fabulous English Tudor mansion in Beverly Hills when I met her. That year she decided to move to the beach where there was "more action." She sold her home at a loss and paid too much for the beach house. She has moved four times in the past five years, always selling at a loss because in her hurry to get to the "fun," she over-buys. Her last house is a modest two-bedroom cottage at Lake Tahoe, where she is now sure "the action is."

Let's analyze these three ladies. Number one is a hard-working woman with a purpose in life. Her move was *toward* something so it was successful. She is happy and fulfilled.

Number two woman moved *away* from something and is haunted. Can you imagine what she goes through? The thought of "someone" finding out about her past! She can not possibly be happy until she is honest with herself. You don't have to broadcast your past, but neither should you pretend it never happened. Her husband, who plans to run for mayor, deserves her total honesty. The longer she pretends, the deeper the valley. And some valleys become so deep they can never be bridged.

And number three, will she ever be happy? Of course not.

19

She moves to move. No matter how many times she moves "the action" is still going to be somewhere else. Wherever *she* is, is the vinegar bottle and life will sour.

Before you move, consider all the advantages and disadvantages. Visit the new area in mind. Talk to people. Investigate. Then be bone honest with yourself. *No* move is better than a bad move. You can always create a new life by creating *more* life. Look around you. The world is your town, too.

QUESTION FOUR

How Do I Let a Man Know I'm Single and Interested in Dating?

When people have known you as a married woman, it is difficult for them to suddenly think of you as single and available. You can't put on a little badge that announces this fact to the world. If you are a divorcée you should take off your wedding ring. As a widow you may not want to remove the band. It's a personal matter.

The first step in announcing your availability is to communicate with your friends, especially those who live some distance away. If you are divorced, rather than widowed, you can be quite candid in your reference to unmarried men they know. If it's a particular man you want to meet, be honest about that, too.

Unlike the never married woman, you may have had your last date ten, twenty, or thirty-five years ago. It's true that our social patterns are in a constant state of flux, but some of the old rules still hold true. You can't just walk up to a man and say, "Why don't you ask me out sometime. I'm divorced now, you know." That is totally awkward and may even permanently discourage a man who might otherwise have been interested.

Another taboo is the schoolgirl trick of asking a friend to hint to him that you're available. You don't need to be that old-fashioned. A better way is to ask one of your married friends to give a dinner party and invite you. Tell her your plan is to call this particular single man who interests you and ask him. If your friend agrees to give the party, be very discreet when you call your prospect. Ask him, as a tremendous favor to you, if he would mind being your escort to a friend's dinner party. Be casual. If he has other plans, thank him and sign off. Whatever you do, don't go into a long description of your divorce or your husband's last illness, your current dating situation, or how much you would like to see him. Unless he is dense beyond words, your simple invitation should tell him you are single and interested in seeing him. It's still the male option as to whether he picks up on it or not.

If you can't convince a friend to give a dinner party, plan one yourself. It doesn't have to be at all elaborate; a casserole buffet or backyard barbecue is perfect. After you have planned your group, call your male friend and say a few people are dropping by, would he care to join you? Most single men love invitations to home-cooked meals. This is almost always an accepted offer. You could ask him by himself, but it seems easier to me to talk to a new man when other people are around, even if all they are is background noise.

Another way to let a man know you're interested in dating him is to buy two tickets to a ball game or to a current play in your town. Then call the gentleman and say you happen to have these two tickets and thought, just by chance, he might like to go with you. Don't tell him how you happen to have the tickets. If he says he's terribly sorry, he would love to have gone, but he can't make it—don't offer to change the tickets. That suggestion should come from him. If it does.t't, ask a girl friend to take one of your children. No need to miss the show!

These little ploys and decoys may seem outmoded and even unnatural by today's new order of things. But remember, it's today's women (not men) who are trying to rearrange the roles. Being forward and overly aggressive isn't going to improve your situation. What you are trying to do is get a chance to know a certain man—better. It's to everyone's advantage if it happens in an easy and acceptable manner.

If you feel you don't know the man in question well enough to call him, you will just have to do some research. Find out where he works, who his friends are, and where his interests lie. If his job is such that you can call him in a business capacity, do so. But have a bonafide reason and expect to be billed for his services. If it requires a visit to his place of business, try to make it at the end of the business day.

Once you determine who this man's friends are, see if you

21

can find some mutual friends. Then try your dinner party idea again, only ask them to have him call you. If this is impossible, ask your mutual friends to take you someplace they know he'll be. From your research about his interests you should be able to plan an encounter, with or without your friends. If he attends a local church, bowls at a certain alley, takes a course at night school, or works avidly for a political party, you should be able to bump into him *someway*.

It's true that dating is an enormous amount of fun, good for your ego, and an accepted way to get to know someone better. But that's all it is. It isn't the determining factor of your happiness, your success or your future. These things are determined by you, not someone who pays your way to the movies. If you truthfully look at the reasons why you want to date, they can be reduced to about seven:

1. To get out and have fun
2. To go where you'll meet other men
3. To prove to yourself you're still attractive to men
4. To show your ex-husband
5. To show your friends
6. To be with a man
7. To get married again

Let's look at these reasons one at a time.
1. *To get out and have fun*
Certainly men are a lot of fun. No question about it. But there is absolutely no rule that says you have to stay home and wait for a man to call before you can go out. Plan your life to include the activities you consider fun. If it's parties, invite people over. If it's theater, museums, or art galleries, go. If it's sports, go.

If you're fun, married couples will like having you around. Plan outings with your family, your children, associates at work. Go! And if necessary, go alone. Once you get over the initial shock of taking yourself somewhere, by yourself, you'll learn to enjoy it—even relish it.
2. *To go where you'll meet other men*
Usually wherever a man takes you on a date, there will be other men there as well. But your chances of meeting them on your own are just as great—even greater. Working at a job you meet men all day long. Pursuing your interests you meet men. The world is

full of men. You'll be more attractive (and accessible) doing what you're doing than hanging on the arm of *another* man.

3. *To prove to yourself you're still attractive to men*

A divorce often leaves a woman in such a self-hate slump that she wonders if she'll ever be any good to any man again. Dating is not the answer to this problem. First you must begin to like yourself again. If you start dating while in a slump, you really won't be attractive to men.

A widow of a thirty-five-year marriage may feel apprehensive of her ability to find another man. She may long desperately for someone to ask her out so she can say to herself, "Yes, I *am* attractive to men." Again, let me say that it is self-defeating to let your dating average determine your attractiveness score. Men can find you utterly fascinating and not be in a position to ask you out. Or you may be in a living cycle where there simply are no available single men. That's why it's imperative that you build a rewarding life for yourself that does not depend on men to make it work.

4. *To show your ex-husband*

Sometimes it's difficult to admit to yourself that you still do care what *he* thinks. Every divorcée has dreamed of walking into a party on the arm of some gorgeous man to find her ex-husband standing there with a scruffy date. That's not an unnatural emotion. But to dwell on it, scheme for it, and allow it to be foremost in your mind is harmful to you and your development as an attractive person.

I do not mean to encourage one-upmanship, but the most impressive "retaliation" is to become an achiever. Success has its own rewards far greater than a dropped jaw at a cocktail party. Success is *good* for you. Concentrate on your life. You are divorced from *him*, remember?

5. *To show your friends*

Again, it's nice to be seen around town with eligible men. But don't force dates on yourself just to impress a few people. Remember, your true friends are your allies and you don't have to fake a full social life for them. Besides, you want your friends to help you meet eligible men. As an unmarried woman you have to learn to be selfish with your time. Spend it where it offers the greatest and longest lasting rewards.

6. *To be with a man*
Obviously there is nothing that can take the place of physical contact with a man. No night school course or pay raise is as exciting as being next to a warm male body, if it is a *meaningful* male body. The longings that overcome you in a celibate life are not the longings for an anonymous act of intercourse. What is missing is the warmth, the feel, the smell, the touch of a man—a man who cares for you and for whom you care.

The theory that women should be able to assume the tomcat role of an evening's cheer to be forgotten about the next morning is not a theory with which most women can live. Why put yourself through sexual encounters for the sake of sex. After all, nothing biologically damaging is going to happen to you if you are *not* participating in an active sex life. You don't *have* to have sexual intercourse to be an alive, feeling woman.

7. *To get married again*
Dating a great many men over a certain period of time doesn't necessarily increase your chances of remarrying. Dating one particular man over the same period of time, should, if indeed it is marriage that you desire. Don't judge your chances of remarrying by the number of men who fill your date book. Be selective in the dates you accept. Your time is valuable. Spend it in building your life, your career, your future. You can tell a great deal more about a man you work with than one who picks up your dinner tab.

Now that you have looked at the reasons for dating, you can see that it's foolish to plan your life around men. You can have a rewarding social life *within* the framework of the life that suits you! Letting a "certain man" know you're free is a fine idea. But if he doesn't pick up on your overture and show interest in you, move on. And *keep* moving. The more interesting things you do and accomplish, the more interesting *you* become. Soon men will be figuring out ways to meet you!

What Are My Chances of Getting Married Again?

According to statistics, among women in the same age brackets, the formerly married woman's chances of remarrying are greater than the never-married woman's chances of marrying for the first time. But that's not a very comforting statistic. If you are a thirty-eight-year-old divorcée, how many never-married women do you know in their late thirties? Not many. However, according to my research, there is a reassuring majority of all divorced and widowed women who do marry again. And often again and even again.

You really should reword this question and ask: "What are my chances of having a truly great second marriage?" To get married again is easy. To make a great marriage is not so easy. If you want to get married again just to get married, I'm sure you can. A woman who has found one husband can usually find another.

If you find yourself in the category of wanting to be married, just to be married, you are certainly not alone. From childhood the female child has been conditioned to becoming a wife and mother. Such training would be fine if the role of wife and mother were presented as an option. Unfortunately the wife-mother role was dangled in front of many of us as the *only* pot of gold at the end of the rainbow. We spent our high school years "going steady" and married the boy we were "going with" in June of our senior year. Or we studied hard to get to college to meet a man. Either way we lost. Gone were all the opportunities that we stumbled over, didn't see, and couldn't handle.

When such a "conditioned" woman finds herself a divorcée or a widow, she flounders. Being alone is frightening. The thought of a job is terrifying. The problem of managing on less money is overwhelming. A twenty-four-year-old career girl would find these situations commonplace. A divorced woman of forty-three or a widow of fifty-eight finds them almost too much to bear.

To get married again then becomes the battle cry of this

formerly married woman. Marriage is what she knows how to do. Marriage is familiar. Marriage seems to be an answer to her immediate problems. Marriage will put her back into the old familiar ruts. In fact, when a woman this desperate to get married finds a new husband, she is often so grateful she will try harder than ever to be a good wife. Hence the common saying, "Second marriages are the best."

Why in the world settle for this? Marriage can be the greatest man-made institution the world has ever known. Or it can be the worst. In between the two poles are where most married people find themselves. Since you are now a single woman why not make a solemn pact with yourself that you will not marry just to be married. Rather you will *only* marry when you are free. By "free" I mean free of the notion that you *have* to get married.

I spent several nights sitting up with a young woman in her tiny apartment in an old remodeled Mediterranean house in the Hollywood Hills. She had announced to me that she was going to marry a man we both knew, who was a film cutter at one of the motion pictures studios. I knew she didn't love him but even more importantly I felt I knew what was behind her sudden decision to marry him.

Claire had been married at sixteen after winning a local beauty contest in Arizona. Quite pregnant, she and her new husband came to California where she found work as an "extra" in motion pictures after the birth of their child. Claire became absolutely stage struck and began taking acting lessons from a woman I knew.

She was twenty-two when I first saw her and very attractive. She had lost the "teen-age beauty queen" look and you knew she was going to become even more attractive in years to come. She was appearing in a workshop production and although her lines were few she gave a memorable performance. She was also in the process of divorcing her husband, who had gone back to Arizona. He refused to send her any money and she was having a difficult time financially.

We had been friends for about three years when she called to tell me she was going to marry Gene. She said she felt this would be the best thing for her and her nine-year-old son, as she could stay home and be a wife and mother. Gene, she said, convinced her to give up this crazy notion of becoming an actress. I told her I wanted to see her and I drove up to her house at 9:00 at night. She was tired and she looked it. For a self-announced bride she also looked most unhappy and despondent.

26

We talked for hours and I tried to point out that because she had not become the famous actress she imagined was no reason to consider marriage as the alternative. I knew she was in a career slump but I also felt she *would* be a success one day soon. Acting is a very precarious occupation and one I would *never* encourage anyone to pursue as a career unless I felt their talent was great. I told Claire this and I am sure that is why she did listen to me. I pointed out that marriage is separate and apart from your success in your chosen field. You don't marry as a way out of working. You don't marry as a way out of trying. Claire was able to admit this and the marriage was postponed.

Claire's story has a happy Hollywood ending. She made a very successful television commercial from which she received enough money to continue her acting career. She eventually made two movies and she did marry again. Her husband is an airline pilot and very supportive of her desire to act. They have a good marriage because they married for the right reasons.

What are the "right reasons" to marry? Surely the top of the list is the desire to share your life with one particular man as he shares his with you. You want to *be* with each other. You love each other. You complement each other. You desire each other. It's an almost impossible task to describe all the right reasons to marry. It's far easier to list the wrong.

At the top of the list of wrong reasons is to marry for an identity. When two people marry, the marriage should be an "addition" to their lives. Not their *very lives*. You don't marry because you're afraid you'll fail in life. You don't marry because you're tired of struggling. You don't marry because you think it's the thing to do.

I don't mean to sound anti-marriage. I'm not. I'm anti bad marriage. There is no need so pressing or void so overpowering or loneliness so staggering which can sanction a bad marriage. Great unions can only live and survive when both partners are emotionally well-balanced and mutually supportive of each other in all endeavors.

You *can* have a great union with a man. But remember that your "chances" of meeting such a man are in direct proportion to the amount of time and effort you put into building the life you now lead. The only thing standing in your way is *you*, and your hesitance to start moving. Don't lower your standards or forsake your goals for a chance to "marry." Men and marriage are not the only answers to living. You've tried marriage. Before you try remarriage, try living.

QUESTION SIX

So Many Couples Live Together Now Without Being Married. Would This Work for Me?

THE FORMERLY MARRIED WOMAN WITHOUT CHILDREN:

When you face a decision in life that rests solely on choice, my sincere advice always, in all things, is do what is best for you. How you live, where you live, and with whom you live are all decisions governed by choice.

To examine this living arrangement, we'll first talk about the formerly married woman without children. I can hardly imagine a man suddenly saying to a woman, "Hey, let's live together," without first indicating that this is on his mind. A man who leaves a couple of clean shirts in your closet, spends the weekend at your home, and buys a supply of his favorite drink, is leaning toward the idea of *something*. If it's living together, don't accept this arrangement until you ask yourself some basic questions.

1. Does he desire this arrangement because he is afraid of marriage?
2. Does he desire this as a mutually beneficial financial arrangement?
3. Does he think of this as a "trial" marriage?

Starting with motive number one, if the man in question has suffered from a bad marriage and is afraid to repeat the performance, honor this. His fears are real, *if* he believes them. What he is suggesting is a "form" of marriage. By eliminating the legal commitments he hopes to eliminate the "bad" part of marriage. In other words he is saying that marriage, as he knew it, is not for him. But if you just lived together and "pretended" it would be all bliss.

You know this is not true. Living together is going to bring out the same problems that marriage would. Proximity causes conflict in any category of living arrangement. Don't siblings fight, and college roommates? All he is eliminating is a legal paper.

He may argue that by eliminating the legal commitment you are creating an atmosphere of mutual trust. You are staying together because you want to stay together. Frankly, I think the woman often stays out of "fear" rather than trust. It is much harder for a woman to move around than a man. Women are basically nesters and the thought of bounding between "living arrangements" is not appealing to most women. To live with the knowledge that he can "split at will" would be more of an enslavement than a freedom.

If his suggestion to live together is based on motive number two, a mutual financial arrangement, I would take another look at this man. Why does he need to share expenses? What is missing in his life? What fear of the future governs him? I am a staunch believer in all women working for any number of reasons: money, self-expression, aid to the community, help for a husband. But I would certainly have little faith in a union based on pooled resources. Where is love? Where is desire? Where is compassion? Tell him to find another man to share his rent. You want to help your loved one, not to sleep with a teammate.

If motive number three governs the man in your life, and he has simply said, "Let's live together and see if it takes, then we'll get married," he has at least made an honest statement. He has voiced his fears that perhaps it won't work. He has stated his intention of marrying you if it does. This is all very sincere. But in no way is it a marriage, trial or otherwise. Marriage is marriage and living together is living together.

No matter how similar the problems that arise in each living arrangement, the solutions and end results are different. Down deep you react as married or *not* married. The notion that you "try harder" in a living-together situation as opposed to marriage, is false. Are you such a pliable person that your personality is dictated by a piece of paper, or lack of it? Are you going to be dear and darling unmarried and a bitch afterward? And what about him? Will he cease to be a loving, caring person if he becomes a husband? Think about it.

After you have examined his reasons for "living together," ask yourself these questions:

1. Am I considering this because it is the only way I can have this man?
2. Am I considering this because I hope it will lead to marriage?
3. Am I considering this because I feel I would prefer this to marriage?

Starting with the first question, if you are considering such a living arrangement because you feel this is the *only* way you can have this man, then the relationship is doomed from the beginning. You are accepting fear into your life and putting "conditions" on your feelings. You are starting life together based on circumstances with which you do not totally agree. This is a poor foundation for future happiness. When you admit such little faith in yourself, how can he have faith in you? Eventually he would come to resent you for being so unprincipled as to agree to a living arrangement that was not what you would have desired.

If you are considering this living arrangement for reason two, hoping it will lead to marriage, you are not being very smart. Why should he ever marry you? Are you going to leave if he doesn't ask you? He can always say you loved him enough to move in, so what has changed? Does your desire for marriage mean you love him more, or less? If marriage is so important, why didn't you insist on it in the beginning? He has all the leverage. You have absolutely no bargaining power. Of course you can always leave but that proves his point, doesn't it? If you want to marry this man my suggestion is *not* to live with him first.

If reason three, living with this man because you think you would prefer this to marriage, is your thinking, then you have the basis to consider it seriously. If you can honestly say to yourself that you are going into this living arrangement with no strings, with no guilt, and with no underlying plans for the future, you will probably have a successful relationship. If you enter with a free spirit, you are able to be your own person, pursue your interests and be supportive of his. Fear is gone. Jealousy is gone. Unhealthy need is gone. Keep it that way. Certainly his needs are to be considered, but not at the expense of your work, your career, your future. Very few things in this world are forever.

If, after all this questioning, you make the decision to live with this man, continually remind yourself that it is not a magic atmosphere which can sustain itself. Very real things happen. He snores and you hang your hose in the bathroom.

He gets cranky when he's hungry and you like to read in bed. It's give and take, tears and triumph, lust and laziness. It's transitory—and temporary.

Remember, moving out is an option open to *both* of you. If at some future date *you* decide you want out, move out. Your life isn't over, or ruined, or senseless. Your life can always take a turn for the better. If the relationship deteriorates, it's better to let it go. You do not have the responsibility to this relationship that you have to marriage. You will receive no financial "reward" for sticking it out. You must think of *your* future and plan for it.

A woman called me on my radio program when I was discussing living arrangements and said she was living with a man and wanted out but had no place to go. She had given up her modeling job and was being supported entirely by him. I asked her where she had worked and she told me she had been a successful free-lance fashion model and done a couple of TV commercials. I suggested that she start immediately to look for work again. She was afraid, she said, because she was older now, had lost her contacts and would need new pictures. I urged her not to give up so easily but to get dressed, put on her face, make a round of the modeling agencies, and talk to people. This at least would be a positive step in the right direction. Her final response to me was that if she worked, her friend would make her move out and she hated to give up the six-room penthouse they share.

How can you encourage a woman to strike out on her own when she is a victim of a "security complex?" The only thing I could do for her was to point out that each day she wasted in worry and inactivity was a day lost. Far better to face the real world and start building a life that features real values. Something is wrong with a man who wants his woman a caged bird. When this beautiful bird begins to age, won't he want a new and fresher friend?

A fear of the future is a genuine fear. But to fear the future and not *do* anything about it, is supremely stupid. This woman's security is not even real. It was based on two sets of neuroses, his and hers. She may think that living in this gorgeous place with all bills paid is Shangri-La. It isn't. Her future depends upon his whims. My final remark to this worried lazy lady was "security isn't a rent-free apartment. Security is owning the building."

The Formerly Married Woman with Children:

All of the foregoing logic applies. Doubly! And further I would add a flat "no" to living with a man not your husband if your children are living at home. Children are group conformists and not very willing to be different. Even the activists in the youth movement in this country today, who scream for individual freedom, are almost boring in their sameness. Your children want to be like other children. What may appear to you as an advanced modern mode of living may be a crushing embarrassment to them. To yourself you're a free spirit. To them, you're freaky.

Living with a man without marriage creates a risky household for children. As they are not his children you are constantly the buffer, worrying that they will displease him, make his life uncomfortable, or be in his way. Not being their stepfather he has no incentive to discipline them, guide them, or even parentally love them. It's an odd situation without properly defined roles.

Conclusion:

Setting the precedent of establishing a home without marriage makes you an easy victim to a senseless, nomadic life. When this relationship ends, what is to prevent the next man you care about from wanting the same "no strings" deal. My feeling is that had marriage been a prerequisite, both parties would have examined the relationship closer. Marriage at least connotes a permanence and responsibility.

A very difficult concept for women to accept is that they *can* have the life they want. The reason most women have unhappy marriages and living arrangements is they "give in" far short of their goals. You have every right to set standards for yourself and then hold to them. When you accept second or third or fourth best, that's exactly what you get.

When I think of "life styles" I'm always reminded of a reception I attended for a newly engaged couple. I was most anxious to meet the bride-to-be because I considered the groom-to-be one of the most attractive young men around. After graduate school he had entered his father's business and was doing exceptionally well. Although he was a boy from tremendous wealth, he was not indulged, lazy, emotionally disturbed or possessed of any of the other traits that often curse a boy in his position. He was any mother's ideal choice for her daughter and I'm sure could have had his pick in the city.

His choice, however, was not a girl from our city at all. He chose a petite brunette who came from a small town and had only been living in the city a short while. She had apprenticed herself to an interior designer and lived in a tiny apartment over his studio. Totally unsophisticated, her dress for the party was sweet but not the least chic when compared to the expensive cocktail dresses, elegant long skirts, and evening pants suits on the female half of the milling throng. I jokingly said to the father of the groom: "I thought this new generation scoffed at marriage. I'm surprised Roger didn't just move her into his apartment." At this the father said to me quite seriously, "You know, I asked him that, and he said he had tried but she thought it was a dumb idea. Apparently he asked her a couple of times but she said it wasn't her way of doing things. Finally Rog decided the only way he was going to get her there was to ask her to marry him and I think he even had to ask her twice!"

If marriage is what you want, marriage is what you should have! Living with someone can be a delightful experience, an exciting adventure, a romantic affair, any number of feelings and sensations. But it's not marriage. Living alone is far better than committing yourself to a shaky living arrangement that simply keeps you out of circulation. Accept the challenge of being single! Plan your life. Pursue your career. Follow your interests. A happy life is far easier to create in a *constructive* atmosphere where *your best interests* are the main attraction.

QUESTION SEVEN

When Should I Have Sexual Intercourse with the Men I Date?

To the young single woman or divorcée in her twenties or early thirties, this may seem like a rather naïve question. But if you are a divorced woman in your forties or a widow in her fifties who grew up amid such moral pronouncements as, "You don't kiss a boy until the third date," this is a very real concern.

As a divorced woman, you receive no social or moral "Behavior Code" with your divorce decree. When you become a widow no one takes you aside to tell you what to expect from new men in your life. You're on your own to work it all out to the best of your ability. If your last date was twenty years ago to your senior prom, you *do* wonder what to do now as a husbandless thirty-eight-year-old-mother of three children. Certainly what works for a single, twenty-two-year-old career girl in New York is not exactly the pattern you should follow.

Whatever your age, as a single woman you want to date and establish a meaningful relationship with a man, or several men. And you should. With each man you date your behavior pattern will differ. It's quite possible (and desirable) to date men of different interests, backgrounds, occupations, and even cultures. Look around. Enter into the dating world with as few preconceived requirements as you can. This is your time to experiment and look objectively at all the options open to you.

To help you find your way sexually at this time in your life, here are some basic guidelines.

1. *Everybody isn't doing it*

   The caricature of the "gay divorcée" and the "willing widow" jumping from bed to bed made for a grand romp in old movies and "Romance" magazines. Equally as unreal is the current cocktail party talk of how everyone is just simply sleeping with everyone nowadays. They're not. You don't have to sleep with the men you date to be modern, popular, or "where it's at."

   It is your option as to whether you accept an overture or whether you decline. Except in the case of involuntary rape, it's still the woman who says yea or nay. There is only *one* reason for engaging in an act of intercourse and that is because *you* want to. Any popularity you hope to gain by being a totally willing and at-random sex partner will be meaningless and temporary.

2. *You won't lose your respectability*

   The other end of the spectrum is to abstain totally from sex out of fear for your reputation. It is *your* life and your decision. If you decide to have intercourse with a man you sincerely care for and who cares for you, you are not going to be branded a promiscuous woman. That is, if you don't flaunt your affair or talk about it indiscreetly.

Your state of mind must always be the determining factor. If it feels right and you can live with it, then it is right for you. Remember, however, the man is bringing his mental and moral attitudes with him to the bed. He may have a more difficult time living with the act than you will. Men were boys reared by mothers and they carry with them always whatever fears, apprehensions, anxieties, obsessions, or taboos mother cared to bestow upon them.

If you find that a man's attitude toward you changes once you have had sexual relations, try to get him to talk about it. If it is impossible for him to communicate the problem to you and the romance ends, be glad. Don't punish yourself by translating his problems into a self-guilt. Whatever his difficulties are, they are his. You are far better off without this man until he has straightened out this thinking. You are not a "ruined" woman for having entered into a sexual communion with this man. You are you.

3. *Your attitude will change*

A divorce leaves you with all nerve ends jangling. Death of a husband is a severe emotional blow. This is not a time to try to set up a behavior pattern. You are quite likely to do any number of things that you will look back upon as foolish, immature, hateful, or even paranoid. This is a time in your life when it is better to do nothing than to jump into situations that require cool judgment. Most women after a divorce or a death are not cool *or* capable of good judgment.

One common reaction for a newly divorced woman is to immediately engage in a very sexual affair. Psychologically you're trying to prove to yourself that you *are* still attractive. The physical closeness of a man "feels good," and you have not felt good for some while. The physical gratification overshadows all else and you are incapable of judging the relationship on any other grounds. If such an affair ends in marriage, it is quite often a disaster.

As you settle into your new life as a formerly married woman you will be more selective in your dating. Proper emphasis will be on you, your children, your job. You will begin to "feel good" for any number of

35

reasons. Dating and being with men will be less frantic. Now your "behavior patterns" will start to form.

As a new widow, don't say to yourself, "I could never love another man." You may think now that this could never happen. But it does, again and again. In fact, widows of great marriages marry sooner than widows of unhappy marriages. It is doing yourself an injustice to set down rules for the future. When you break these rules you will feel guilt, and you don't need to add this new problem to your life.

Accept the idea of seeing other men when the time comes. Enter into the social world with an open mind and an open heart. In time you should find yourself drawing closer and closer to one man. Naturally the physical side of the relationship will become more intense. As an alive human being you will want this man totally—and you should. It's normal, it's healthy, it's exciting, it's life.

4. *Choose your place carefully*
If you are a formerly married woman with children, don't use your home as the trysting place if the children are in residence. It is an unfair circumstance to make them face. How you conduct your life is, of course, your business. You, however, have a responsibility as a mother. Often you will find *you the mother* in conflict with *you the woman*. In any situation you must always do what is best for the children.

Teen-agers have one code of ethics they apply to themselves and one they apply to their parents. Don't think that because your children are older they will accept and understand more readily. They won't. Children of all ages want their parents to be parents. Part of the responsibility of being a parent is to behave like one.

If the children are away for the weekend, and you and the man in your life want to stay together at your home, just keep a few things in mind. If your neighborhood is close and nosy you may be letting yourself in for unnecessary heartache. People are cruel. Unhappily married women who are totally envious of the life you lead are especially cruel. Unwilling or unable to change their situations, they will not miss an opportunity to take a swipe at yours. Not all women are like this of course, but enough are to make it worth your while to find another meeting place.

If you choose to go to his apartment, don't start rearranging the furniture. It's fine to cook and do dishes but leave the dirty shower alone. Make love and have fun. Don't play house. Let him know you're there to be with him.

CONCLUSION:

The only time to have intercourse with a man is when it's meaningful and it is what *you* want to do. If you sincerely care about a man and he cares about you, then it is time to say with your body what you feel in your heart.

QUESTION EIGHT

Should I Take the "Pill" Just in Case?

Medically I am not qualified to answer as to your physical ability to take birth control pills. I highly recommend that you see your doctor for an examination before you put anything chemical into your body. If you took the pills during your first marriage with no ill effects, there is probably no reason you can't continue to take them now—if you need to.

If you have never taken the pill and find yourself in a heavy relationship with the fear of pregnancy hanging over your head, by all means go to your doctor and talk to him. If you would rather not go to him, contact the nearest office of Planned Parenthood. They will supply you with the latest material on the subject of birth control and arrange for you to have an examination by one of their doctors. Planned Parenthood is strictly an information bureau dedicated to the best interest of all society.

To take the pill "just in case" you decide to have sexual intercourse with "someone" smacks of moral insensibility. In this instance I am using the word "moral" as your personal standard as to what is right for you and what is wrong for you. Ultimately you are the final judge as to what you can live with and what you cannot. Therefore I feel to take the pill when you are not having a meaningful relationship with one certain man is a self-degrading operation. You are in essence offering yourself to any man, making no moral distinction between them.

Sex, to be special, must be enjoyed with someone special. And the responsibility should be shared equally. Certainly you are showing you care by arranging to take birth control pills. He should show his care and feeling by the attitude he takes toward you. There should be no doubt in your mind that this man is not simply interested in sex, but in the whole you.

One way to answer the question of the pill is to consider what you would tell a teen-age daughter. Would you arm her with the pill just in case? Or would you try to help her develop a set of values that would enable her to make her own decisions? The fear of loss of reputation or "wicked sinner" syndrome should never be held over the head of a female child. But neither should you say, "Here's the pill, enjoy." Keeping the lines of communications open with a daughter, you can, with understanding, help her make decisions. The services of Planned Parenthood, by the way, are also available to teen-agers.

There is nothing easy about being a formerly married woman. You are super-sensitive to criticism, censure, and public opinion. You over-think, over-react, over-punish. There are times when you are convinced your life is ruined forever. You can't isolate the act of intercourse from a moral evaluation no matter how hard you try. Consciously or subconsciously your life is made up of constant self-judgments. The only way to build-in a new feeling of worth is to keep telling yourself that you are learning and will *continue* to learn. You will develop your own behavior code. You will build a life that works for you. You will not accept the ordinary when the extraordinary is possible.

If you are still undecided about the pill, do this. Go to your doctor and find out all about the pill. Buy them and put them in your dresser drawer. When you are going with someone you care a great deal about, start taking the pills. You should not take the pill "just in case" someone suggests you go to bed with them. You are the master of your passions, a person of worth and merit. You do not gain anything but heartache by accepting a behavior code that doesn't fit in with your picture of you.

I Am in Love with a Man Who Just Doesn't Have a Strong Sexual Drive. Is There Something Wrong with Him - or with Me?

Asking this question indicates you feel an inadequacy in yourself or the man in question. Or both. Either you have need of a more active sex life or you aren't enjoying the one you have. Or again, a combination of the two. Let's look at the circumstances that could cause you to question your sexual relationship with the man you love. For love must be the basis of a great sexual union or we've found one cause of the trouble. Assuming love is present in both parties, something else must be amiss.

1. *The frequency norm*

It is impossible for anyone to decide arbitrarily how many acts of intercourse should take place within a given time in order for a relationship to be "normal." If you set up a "quota" in your mind and start counting, this would indicate you are looking for reasons to fault the relationship. Acts of intercourse must be naturally motivated, not a duty performed.

A frequency norm based upon past experiences, habits of friends, or an imaginary figure serves no purpose whatsoever. Each relationship should be as individual as the partners. A relationship that is healthy should not be static with "certain days" and "certain times."

2. *Who is the initiator*

If you feel that you would enjoy more time spent in lovemaking, initiate it. Too many women mope around wondering why the men in their lives don't make love to them more often. A simple solution to their problems would be to make the overture them-

39

selves. There is no rule that states a woman must wait until she's tapped on the shoulder.

It is not wanton to want to make love. It's healthy, normal, satisfying, and very much a part of life. What is wrong is to hide it, dwell on it, and feel inadequate when it doesn't happen. Show your desire by reaching out to him. You be the one to untie his bathrobe and pull him back to bed. His lack of a sex drive may be your apparent lack of interest.

3. *Timing and circumstances*

A formerly married woman often forgets that she is that—an unmarried woman. In a nonmarriage relationship with a man you are dealing with an element of timing that is not usual. Lovemaking must be arranged to fit in with jobs, children, and geography, all of which can and does contribute to the infrequency of time alone. This is another way the woman can make the overture. By arranging your life to contain quiet pockets of alone-time you are saying, "I am here and I want you."

4. *His mental state*

Attitudes become a primary factor in lovemaking. If you do have children, you are a mother in his eyes. His desire for you as a woman can be in conflict with his moral concern for your situation. It's impossible to know exactly how a man was reared, what early moral training he brings into the relationship, what battles he may be fighting in his head. Naturally all these things come with him to the bedroom.

A man also brings to the bedroom his past and present experience. He may have had a devastating marriage that left him with little self-confidence in the field of lovemaking. He may hesitate to reach out for fear of rejection. He may be concerned that his performance will be less than adequate. Again, you have no knowledge of his mental state about his sex life.

A man may be going through a very difficult transition in his job or business life. He may feel, because you are not his wife, that he should not discuss his problems or worries with you. He may feel hesitant to burden you when you have so many problems of your own. A man with mental anguish is not always a good sex partner. But that doesn't mean he lacks a sex drive.

I watched a man become a sloppy drunk due to his

wife's insensibilities in this area. At a dinner party one night, after many, many drinks, I asked this man why he was doing this to himself. His answer was, "Because it gives me an excuse for not making love to my darling wife." His tone was bitter and his attitude quite nasty. "Come on, Vern," I said, "make sense. You love Gloria very much." He took another swallow of his brandy and laughed, "Sure I love her, but if you can't get it up, you can't get it up." I knew their marriage had not started out this way three years ago, and I asked him what was wrong. His explanation made things crystal clear. "My performance as a sex partner is a barometer of my business. Good days I'm good, bad days I'm no good. Gloria thinks there's something wrong with me. She's got me so psyched now I don't know if I'll ever get it up again."

A sad story? You bet. Here is a man who got drunk to have an excuse for not being able to make love to his wife. Instead of trying to understand her husband's body chemistry, Gloria preferred to place blame. And in her blame placing she actually forced the situation she feared.

5. *His physical state*

A tired man does not make a good sex partner. Again, this doesn't mean he lacks a sex drive. You have no way of knowing the state of a man's health. Perhaps he has low blood sugar or a thyroid condition. A man who is perpetually tired should be encouraged to have a medical checkup. Show compassion for his needs rather than dwelling on your own.

It's so terribly important to withhold judgments. The physical side of the relationship will grow just as magnificently as the mental and spiritual sides. But you must help each other. He should accept and work with your attitudes toward sex just as you accept and work with his. When you show common concern for the whole man, mental and physical, you will have just that—a *whole* man.

6. *A low sex profile*

Sex is a form of energy derived from a specific feeling. Contrary to some current novels, movies, and TV dramas, our male population is *not* made up entirely of cocksmen. There are some men who just don't seek a great deal of sex and there is nothing about their manhood that needs questioning.

41

In particular, I can think of a doctor I know who is an accomplished violinist, a knowledgeable ornithologist, and an expert on Poe. His wife has told me that engrossed in any of these fascinating interests, he is totally unaware of her presence. She said she could pose in front of the fire in a see-through negligee and his head would not turn.

This wife is smart enough not to question her desirability. She knows she would make herself miserable. If she were to judge herself by slick-magazine terms she would turn in her feminine hygiene spray. There is nothing "wrong" with either one of them. She understands his interests and his needs, and doesn't create unreal problems. When they desire each other sexually, they say so.

Before you start questioning yourself or the man in your life, consider what he finds entertaining, exciting, fascinating. Perhaps you have some genuine competition for his attention. Accept it, and find something that fascinates you. You cannot drape yourself over his chair *all* the time.

7. *Comparisons*

It is very difficult not to make comparisons in life. In some ways all our growth is based on systematic comparison. But there are some instances when comparison is not only unfair but works to our disadvantage. Lovemaking falls into this category. Because of the element of love, it is impossible to make a cold rational judgment of a man's ability as a sex partner. Your findings can only be based on experience and these experiences themselves are influenced by love, or the lack of it. Love, whatever it is, is the one element science can't chart.

What you can chart, or react to, is the orgasm or climax that does or does not accompany the act of intercourse. This is where comparison does flourish. If a woman has had a sex partner who evoked an earth-shaking orgasm in her, she will always compare this experience with future encounters, whether or not love is present.

If you are a woman who has had a great sexual experience but find it missing in your present relationship, you must freely discuss it with him. Don't mentally make the comparison while going through the motions feeling frustrated and a martyr. It's totally unfair to the man in your life who, with your help, could quite possibly become a great lover.

THE DESIRED RESULTS

To go back to your original question, there is probably nothing wrong with either of you that couldn't be cured by a good honest discussion. Take into account all the factors I have mentioned and then be very truthful with him. Ask him questions about his needs and tell him yours. Tell him you love him and you want to feel that he loves you. Tell him you love him sitting across the dinner table from you but you also love him when you are closely held and gently touched.

QUESTION TEN

I Know There Must Be More to Sexual Intercourse Than I've Experienced. How Do I Tell This to a Man?

While interviewing marriage counselors in the research for this book, I had a very frank discussion with a woman in one of our California Courts of Conciliation. "Sexual ignorance," she said, "causes more divorce than any single item. I mean sexual ignorance on the part of the men. Too many women have punching-bag sexual relations with their husbands. Few men take time to learn about women, their physiology, their needs, their functions. It's on and off and see you in the morning."

Biologically it is possible for every woman to have an orgasm. If you do not know what I am talking about, you have never had one. Some women have lived a lifetime and given birth to several children without sharing this experience with the man in their life. Why? Because it takes a knowledgeable lover to bring a woman to her climax. If you feel "left out" in your sexual relations with the man in your life, then it is because you are not reaching a climax. This is the gnawing feeling inside you that keeps saying "something is missing."

How do you tell this to a man? You first go to the library and get two or three basic books on sex. Privately you read them thoroughly. Buy the book you feel is the most informative. Mark passages you would like *him* to read. Most particularly underline the word *clitoris* and its function. Too many men don't know what the woman's clitoris is, where it is, or what to do about it!

The next step is to tell the man in your life that you want to talk to him. This is not a discussion to be conducted at the dinner table, over the phone, or on the way home from the movies. This discussion is to take place in bed, propped up on pillows and helped along by a cold bottle of champagne or a pitcher of martinis. It's up to you to arrange your schedule so this can be an uninterrupted evening.

Take to bed with you the book you have carefully marked. Tell him how much you enjoyed reading about men. Tell him you decided you were just not as informed as you should be and you wanted to be a great sex partner. Then say to him that he might like to read about you. If he seems offended tell him you simply wanted to have a good talk about sex. Don't let him hedge. Start by asking him a question about men that has always puzzled you. Tell him you want to experiment. Explore his body. I can't imagine any man who wouldn't take it from here.

You are not warped, you're real! Don't feel that this is wrong, dishonest, or dirty. It's natural. It's life. It's love. I have seen many marriages dissolve which I felt could have been saved if the partners had genuinely talked to each other in this way. I see marriages every day that could be improved enormously by a good dose of basic sex honesty. You can't cure problems by banishing them to some secret place in your body. They will grow, fester, and soon destroy the good things.

Many of us grew up in an environment where discussions on sex were nonexistent. We formed our notions from scraps of conversations, older brothers and sisters, books and the movies—hardly what one would call a desirable course of instruction. We entered into marriage based on unreal courtships and proceeded to learn about life on a trial-and-error basis. Many of us accepted the passive role of the unsatisfied wife because we simply didn't know any differently.

You can change all that now. You can seek sexual satisfaction. Work as a partner with the man in your life. No relationship should remain static. Love is alive and as a living thing it moves, grows, advances, and blossoms. So should you.

QUESTION ELEVEN

How Can I Distinguish Between Perverted Sex and the "Norm"?

To feel "perversion" in sex is to feel repulsion, to feel you are doing something against your better judgment. It is a totally mental reaction to a physical act. When we take all our past moral training, spiritual understanding, parental guidance, and mix it together with current thought, books we've read, movies we've seen and remembrances of our actual past experiences in sex, we form an incredible mish-mash that is *"our pronouncement"* of what is perverted and what is not.

No sexual act between two willing participants should be labeled perverted. If one partner "goes along" with a sexual practice that he or she deems "perverted," then in that person's mind it is. No other thinking matters but your own. Therefore your thinking must change if you feel your attitude should change. To continue to participate in a sexual act you cannot accept as normal is indeed perversion.

No sexual relationship starts out with all systems "go." The woman is usually carried along on the sheer wave of excitement. She enjoys the caressing and the intimacy of physical nearness. In rare instances does she immediately reach her full enjoyment potential. As the relationship continues, it should be refined. There is absolutely nothing perverted in wanting all there is to sex. That is why communication between the partners is essential. Not talking about your feelings is one of the greatest deterrents to a fulfilling sex life.

By talking about your sexual reactions I don't mean that each separate step in lovemaking should be commented upon, outlined, and analyzed. You can over-talk the subject and make it too clinical. You should indicate what you like and what helps to bring you to your climax. You should also be doing the actions he likes, and doing them with no feelings of repulsion or guilt.

If you feel you (or your partner) are not sufficiently knowledgeable in lovemaking, go to the bookstore or library and get two or three of the new sex manuals. They are very basic and enormously informative. Read them together or separately—but read them. Again, this is *not* a perversion—it's a quest for knowledge. The more knowledge you have on any subject the greater will be your understanding. As you understand your body and your basic desires you will be less quick to judge an act as perverted or unnatural.

Apart from, but primary to, the act of lovemaking, is your state of mind at the time. In order not to feel a sense of worthlessness (which is a perversion) the relationship must have an aura of love around it. You must feel he cares for you and he must feel that you in turn care about him. Unless this premise exists you will constantly be in conflict with that small voice within you—your conscience.

To engage in isolated acts of intercourse with a variety of men just as part of the evening's entertainment would indicate perversion. Ask yourself why you do this? Is it an insecurity on your part that a man won't "like" you if you don't? Is it done in a desire to be modern, free, and uninhibited? Whatever the reason, it is not good for you, your psyche, or your future ability to have a great sexual union with one man. It isn't the moral pronouncements of others that make it a perversion, but the lack of self-love it indicates. To love another you must first love yourself. To have a great love life you must love yourself, your partner, and what you're doing.

Location is another factor that enters into lovemaking. If you have children, certainly they must be considered. That is why I stress again and again—don't use your home as a love nest when the children are in residence. If they were to discover you in an intimate act, lasting damage could be done to them, to you, and to the man. With all the alternate locations available, it would be "perverted" to choose the couch in your living room.

Personally I feel that the modern tendency to put sex under a microscope, on book jackets, in Vista-Vision and grammar school classrooms indicates an obsession with sex that is itself a perversion. Removing the elements of mystery, suggestion, romance, and love leaves you a very naked thing indeed. While it's helpful to have a marriage manual as a road map, you don't need colored illustrations at every street corner.

Sex is very personal and as unique and individual as the two participants. What works for someone else is not necessarily going to work for you. But what does work for you is not a perversion, no matter how basic, bizarre, or "unnatural" it may be judged by "others." *Others* aren't doing it, you and the man you love are. Other values, other morals, other opinions have no place in your boudoir. Final judgment in sex, as in every other action in life, is yours. If you like what you're doing, do it!

QUESTION TWELVE

My Religion Forbids Remarriage and the Pill. But I Am Still Young— What Should I Do?

It is very tempting to say, "embrace another religion," but this, of course, is no answer to your problem. I am also tempted to duck the question entirely because it deals with theology, and theology is one area in which it is terribly difficult to give advice. I will answer your question, but please keep in mind that this answer is based on what I believe and what I feel is right. Whether this advice works for you is, of course, up to you and your understanding of theology.

You are in a contest between your head and your genes, your heart, and your glands. Nature is on the side of your basic needs, cravings, and desires. Nature knows no religion, accepts no dogma, recognizes no creeds. In other words you are a young, vital woman with very natural instincts who carries around a set of rules saying, "No, no, no."

You are in torment because of what you were *taught* to *believe*. Your fears are not based on a philosophy *you* evolved, but rather on a set of rules or standards you have accepted. In accepting these rules you have also accepted the punishment factor that goes along with them. You now fear that if you deviate from the tenets of your religion you will suffer dire consequences. And so you will. Your *thinking* is the only mechanism that can set you free just as your thinking is now the chain that binds you. Your total battle begins and ends in your head. Only you can punish you.

As a living being we are governed by three sets of rules.

1. *Natural laws:* These laws, inherent in all life, say we must eat, breathe, sleep, move around—or we'll die. These rules never vary.
2. *Man-made laws:* All of your day-to-day living is regulated by laws society sets forth to govern the con- duct of its members. These laws are made by people or changed by people.
3. *Personal laws:* To a certain degree all members of society govern themselves in the area of choice. This is called our personal conduct. These laws we make up ourselves.

Natural laws we cannot change. Personal and man-made laws we can. Your marriage was according to a man-made law. When the marriage was over you dissolved it according to a man-made law. You didn't turn off your desires, needs, or wants. They are still with you and very much a part of you. These are *natural* instincts that follow right along with our desire for food, clothing, and shelter.

Now, as a young divorced woman with strong religious convictions and equally strong natural desires, you are at war with yourself. The same religious ethic that forbids remarriage certainly does not encourage at-random sex with a variety of partners. Nor does it suggest you live with one man without the benefit of marriage. What alternative does it leave you? Abstinence and the inability to completely relate to a man. Unless, of course, you can find a male counterpart who will settle for a platonic friendship with no hope of marriage.

I am not making fun of the situation, I am simply trying to show how religion, which is entirely conceived by man, can hamstring us beyond belief. What I would suggest to you is that you make no determination at this time. Date whomever appeals to you and quit thinking about remarriage. When you find one man with whom you would like to have a total relationship, do so—again without making any decisions.

One of the strongest female fantasies we apply to a relationship with a man is that "We're going to get married." When we say that audibly or to ourselves, it seems to make everything all right. It helps soothe our heavy conscience. It rights the balance of behavior. It makes it easier for us to live with ourselves. Going into a relationship saying, "We're not going to get married" is equally as unreal. Just put one foot in front of the other. Enjoy the feelings, emotions, and joys. Make no judgment—until it's time to make a decision.

If the subject of marriage comes up you will be better equipped to make your evaluation. You can't expect to force your religious beliefs on another. If the man in question is willing to continue the relationship without benefit of marriage, you won't have to make a decision. If he isn't, you will. Here it becomes a private matter between you and your religion. Just remember, all things change. Rules and codes of behavior decided upon hundreds of years ago were put together to fit *those* times. The laws of our country, your country, allow marriage, divorce, and remarriage.

When I conducted my radio program in Los Angeles, I was on the air on weekends. The Sunday morning shows often evolved into religious discussions. The question of remarriage was a great favorite. One morning a woman called in and said she had been divorced at twenty-five and didn't remarry until forty-three because of her religious convictions. I asked her why then at forty-three did she decide to marry. Her father died, she told the radio audience, and she realized it was *his* censure, rather than God's, she feared. All these years she had said she couldn't marry because of her church, and she actually thought she meant it.

I asked her how she felt about her religion now that she was remarried. She said she was completely happy for the first time in her life. "God," she said, "would understand and be glad for me." With the death of her father went fear and threat of punishment. "I'll take my chances with God any day," she said, and hung up the phone.

A question all of us might ask ourselves is: Where is our faith? In religion or in God?

LET'S TALK ABOUT THE PILL:

A religion that forbids birth control pills, or any form of contraception, is refusing to recognize the desperate need of the world to control its population. The scary facts are in any modern textbook, heavily and scientifically documented. It is not wrong to question the tenets of your religion. Religion should be a living faith that advances with the people to answer all their spiritual needs.

No matter how many arguments you have with yourself, it is quite probable you, as a young woman, will have sexual relations with a man. (And you should!) If this union results in an unwanted pregnancy, you have created a still greater problem. And abortion is a far more drastic solution to pregnancy than contraception.

RELIGION AND LIFE:

In an age of lessening morals and elastic standards I don't like to recommend that anyone break the tenets of her religion. Faith in a higher order of things is a most desirable attitude. After all, there is a certain satisfaction, joy, and comfort that comes from adhering to the tenets of one's religion. Unhappiness occurs when religion and life are in conflict.

In religion, the final decision is always, in all matters, yours. Do what you can live with comfortably. Don't set unrealistic standards.

QUESTION THIRTEEN

I Am Going Quite Steady with a Man. Is It Wrong for Him to Occasionally Spend the Night at My Home?

1. The answer to this question depends first upon your living arrangements.
   a. *If you live alone*

   As a divorced or widowed woman living alone, either in an apartment or a home, you are free to conduct your life any way you wish. After all, the only person you are answering to is you. If you feel you would like the man in your life to stay over at your residence, and he wants to, go ahead.

   However, I wouldn't convey the fact to friends, neighbors, or the girls at work. Your private life should be just that—private. You should also insist that he not answer the phone or go after the paper in a robe.

   If you live in a small community where your

comings and goings are obvious to friends and neighbors, consider the elements of gossip. As distasteful as gossip is, it still exists and can inflict damage. Certainly you are living your own life and following your own sense of right and wrong, but flaunting it in an atmosphere where it can do harm is certainly not to your advantage. Be smart. Learn to live—but also let live.

b. *If you live with a roommate*

When two women live together they should have a few house rules decided in advance. One of the first rules to formulate is the question of overnight male guests. This prevents unfortunate scenes that could be damaging all around. A confrontation in the bath between your male friend and your uninformed roommate could be disasterous. In fairness to all, the intimately involved persons should know your plans in advance. He should know about her. She should know about him.

If your roommate is out of town for the weekend you should be free to entertain the way you see fit. If she returns unexpectedly, be prepared in advance. It's her apartment, not his, and it's his obligation, and yours, to make room for her. Learn to think through situations before they happen. Consider the pros and cons. Life becomes easier when you chart your course and don't live in a hit-or-miss style.

c. *If you live with your family*

I can see no reason, outside of dire emergency, for a male guest to spend the night with you at your parents' home. And if you live with your parents it is their home. When you live under their roof you live under their laws.

Even if you don't live with your family, they are a factor. If you live in the same community you certainly don't want to bring them unnecessary grief. That's why your living pattern should be your private business. If everything you do is "common knowledge," it could filter back to them and cause them some unhappy moments. Certainly it's "your life" but living it should never bring harm to others when it can be avoided.

d. *If you have children at home*

As a formerly married woman with children, you

find yourself in conflict. You the woman versus you the mother. Ideally there should be no conflict, but this is hard to manage. Frankly, I say No to a man spending the night with the children there. Find another time, another place.

Your children are your responsibility. Their character development is your sacred trust. Life, to children of divorce, is all too soon a series of unanswered questions. A parent's feeble attempt at words of explanation seldom satisfies. "My father's gone. Why?" You know why. Or think you know. But explanation is nearly impossible.

Why create a situation that can only add to the confusion? Why let a man who is not your husband, not their father, have access to your bedroom? Certainly he is there because he likes you and you like him. When he leaves is it because he no longer likes you? When a "new friend" appears, what do you say? Your nine-year-old daughter will one day be sixteen and bringing home her boyfriend who likes her. What is your rule going to be? Upon what will she base her personal behavior pattern? Think ahead. Never let "the woman" over-rule "the mother." Both can, and should, have their special times.

Carefully, as you plan, incidents sometimes do occur. When they do try to make the best of them without raising questions of guilt, losing tempers or telling lies. A woman wrote me from Texas about how her two teen-age daughters had come home from a weekend outing early Sunday morning rather than Sunday afternoon as expected. She and her beau woke up to see the girls standing over her bed, wide-eyed. "You got married!" exclaimed one of the daughters. Before the mother could think of anything to say, her friend sleepily raised his head and said "No, we're just practicing."

Since the two actually were in a heavy relationship, the man moved in his things that day and three months later they were married. It was a solution which fortunately worked, but it could have been drastic. Had the mother shouted and told them to get out or had the man left in anger, it could have been a tragic end to friendship all the way around. Even at the end of the three months' trial, had the man moved out, it was still a better way to handle the situation.

Another case history with the opposite result is one I heard years ago when I was almost too young to properly understand. It happened to a girl in our neighborhood and caused a great deal of comment among the mothers. A thirteen-year-old girl came home from school one noon and found her mother and a man, undressed, in an intimate position on the living room couch. Two weeks later the mother found the daughter in her bedroom repeating the performance with a neighbor boy. Two months later the little girl was in the hospital getting an abortion!

The girl went away to boarding school for the next few years. I didn't hear about her again until she was seventeen, at which time she ran away with a boy to Nevada and was married. The mother promptly had the marriage annulled and sent the girl to live with her father. I understand she married again at nineteen, had two children, but is back living with her father because her husband left her.

I feel the mother's rejection of the girl after her abortion was what rushed her in the unhappy direction her life took. Wasn't she in essence being punished for the very act her mother had committed? We constantly urge our children, "Grow up, be a man, act like a lady." If this is indeed what we want it is our responsibility to be grown up ourselves. Training by example is far more effective than constant nagging, lectures, or banishment.

2. The second major consideration is *your* mental attitude.

To spend the night with the man in your life in your home may appeal as the most natural thing in the world. It could be or it could just as easily *not* be. Your mental attitude is the prime determinator. If his presence overnight makes you worried or uneasy, then it would be far wiser to find another meeting place. Be honest with him and say you would rather go somewhere else. This is your home, your life, and your decision. If this man cares for you as much as you think he does, he will be understanding *and* cooperative.

You don't need to explain or justify your decision. The sooner you learn to speak up about your feelings, the sooner you will be in control of your own life. Being in control removes the fear surrounding so many relationships. You must never go against your better judgment because you're "afraid of losing him." Giving into fear keeps it fat and happy and on your back forever.

To a great many people home is sacred. Home is where you are completely you, barriers down, facades off. Home is your refuge, your nest, your domain. Home is the center from which you go forth, day after day. How you treat your home *is* important.

How he treats your home is equally important. And he'll take his cue from you. If you treat it as a convenient place to keep a few things, eat a meal, and spend the night—so will he. If you take care of it, make it pleasing, treat it kindly—so will he. If it's special for you it will be special for him.

I have seen a couple of magazine articles on what the thoughtful single girl keeps in the bathroom for male guests. My personal feeling is that this is a bit too studied. It's one thing to lend him your razor, but to have shaving lotion, an unopened toothbrush, strong spray deodorant, and an extra-large terry cloth robe is letting yourself in for all kinds of suspicions.

More to the point is what we talked about earlier. Your home has a distinct place in your life. You and your home have a distinct place in the community. When a man comes into your home it is at your invitation and under your code of behavior. If the relationship ends, you will be living there after he's gone.

Earning your own living (or part of it) and running your own house is not the easiest thing in the world. Everyone, and most especially the man in your life, will have greater respect for you if you respect the place where you live.

3. The last consideration is *his* mental attitude.
   The suggestion that the man in your life spend the night at your home should come from him. Even though the invitation is yours, the overture should be his. To blatantly state, "Let's go to my house," robs him of the male initiative.

   Traditionally man takes woman to his cave. But if your digs are more attractive, your larder better stocked, and your bed sheets fresher, he will undoubtedly make the suggestion to "stay over." Nevertheless, the final invitation is yours.

Some men, however, are just not comfortable in a woman's bed. If the man in your life is hesitant or uneasy about staying with you, don't urge him. He has his own set of values. Forcing him into a situation that goes against his way of thinking could harm the relationship. He may feel that staying at your home is embarrassing or unmasculine for any number of private reasons that are his to live with.

Taking all these factors into consideration, it is not wrong for the man in your life to spend the night in your bed—unless you think it is wrong. Think through all the situations I've mentioned and see where your living pattern fits. Then make your decision based on what's best for you! It's your life, your home, and most particularly, YOUR BED.

QUESTION FOURTEEN

What Do I Tell My Children When I Go Away for the Weekend with a Man?

This of course, depends entirely on the age of the children. If they are young children, say under the age of seven or eight, you don't really have to tell them anything but "good-bye." It is imperative, however, that the baby-sitter or person in charge know where you are going. If you haven't decided on an exact location before you leave, call home the minute you choose a place to spend the night. Give the sitter the number and tell her how you are listed. This is one area in which you shouldn't play games. You must be reachable when you leave your children in someone's charge.

If your children are over eight you will have to tell them something. My advice is to say you are going on a tiny vacation and you'll see them Sunday night. Don't over-explain, make up wild excuses, or tell them the bare facts. It's unfair to complicate their lives unnecessarily. Also, you don't want them to know things that you would rather keep quiet. You can't tell a child a "secret" and then say, "Don't tell your father or grandmother." The children didn't create your situation, you did. It's up to you to keep their world as "normal" as you can.

Again, tell the person in charge where you will be and how you can be reached. But tell her in private. Arrange to meet the man in your life away from your home. If he has to pick you up, try to arrange it so he arrives Friday before the children are home from school, or after they have gone to bed. You can say good-bye to them in the morning before they leave for school. If he absolutely must pick you up when the children are around, don't go into a wild explanation of how he is just taking you to the airport or train station. Simply say good-bye.

If your children are teen-agers they will have the whole caper pegged anyway. The moment you say you're going to be gone for the weekend, they will have a fairly accurate idea of what's happening. If you are leaving one of your older children in charge, he or she will have to know how to reach you. This situation demands confidence between the two of you. When you leave one child in charge, that child should feel the responsibility. You should make it clear to all members of the household who's in charge and what is expected of each of them.

I don't recommend leaving children of any age in charge of the house if it can be avoided. It would be far wiser to plan your weekend away to coincide with the weekend they are going to visit their father or some other relative. You will have a much better time if you aren't constantly worrying about where they are and what they're doing.

It may seem now, if you have small children, as if you'll *never* have time to slip away. Believe me, you will. By thinking ahead and making plans in advance, you can fit any activity into your life that you deem meaningful. Going away on the spur of the moment is fine if your children are properly supervised and you know everything is under control. But to drop everything when a man says "let's go" is wrong for several reasons.

I have lately watched a very attractive divorcée in the process of destroying herself and hurting her children. She is traveling with a professional athlete and leaving her two daughters with a college girl to run the house. She is gone at least two weeks a month. When I last saw her she had new dark circles under her eyes and a franticness that was alarming. She insists that she is doing the only thing she can do.

She wants desperately to marry this man and is afraid not to go wherever he goes. Yet I know the mother instinct in her is taking its toll in sleepless nights and causing the hollowness around her wildly darting eyes.

If you have children, your first responsibility is to them. I'm sorry, but I don't buy the selfish whimper, "I owe this to myself." If what you do harms your children you owe it to yourself *not* to do it. I don't mean that you must devote every waking moment to your children. That is stifling to you *and* the children. Certainly a woman has definite needs, but these needs should be a *part* of life, not the dominate feature. Any man who truly cares for you is going to understand (and applaud) your statement that you can't leave this weekend because you have a Little League game to attend, a formal to buy for your daughter, and no reliable sitter. You can add to your statement, ". . . but I think we could work something out for next weekend." After all, he has only himself to think about while your world is many-peopled.

It is still a man's world in that the men do the choosing and the asking. However, you don't have to do what *any* man says unless it is exactly what you want to do. Try and rid yourself of the ridiculous fear so many women carry from childhood that taunts: "He won't like me if I don't do what he wants." Pleasing a man is delightful. Pleasing a man at the expense of your children is not good for you, for him, or for them. *You* are the head of your household. Accept your responsibility with joy and confidence.

QUESTION FIFTEEN

I Have Reason to Believe My Ex-Husband Has Homosexual Tendencies. Should I Stop His Visitation Privileges with Our Children?

All visitations rights and privileges are handled by the court. It is impossible for you to stop your husband from seeing the children unless you bring the matter to your lawyer and ultimately to court.

But before you take that step, look long and hard at your suspicions. Unless your ex-husband is a self-admitted homosexual openly living with another man, the only thing you have to go on *is* your suspicions, hearsay, rumor, or hunches. To point an accusing finger at any man based on these assumptions is a very dangerous and damaging thing.

Let's look at the reasons women have given who suspected their ex-husbands of homosexual tendencies.

1. *An unsatisfactory sex life in marriage*

Of the hundreds of divorced women I have talked to, nearly all complained of an erratic, unsatisfactory, or nonexistent sex life. The most common complaint is: "He never touched me. Days would go by without any lovemaking of any kind." Of the women I have interviewed in depth, my conclusion is that they were seldom satisfied. To someone with an active, healthy, satisfying sex life this may sound preposterous. It isn't. Here statistics do back me up.

It is not unusual for such an unsatisfied woman to think that something "must be wrong" with her husband.* It is painful to believe the trouble may be in ourselves. Wherever the trouble lies, the least likely place is a latent homosexuality in the husband.

2. *A suspicion of the "group" your ex-husband has for friends*

A divorced woman is often super-critical of her ex-husband's new life. Since it is much easier for a man to build a new social life, an ex-wife often sits back in wonder as her husband begins surrounding himself with activity and people. In a jealous pique, how easy to point a finger at a homosexual member of the crowd and say, "He *must* be one also, he hangs around with them." How ridiculous. In today's society nearly everyone knows (or thinks he knows) a homosexual.

It is often difficult for certain women to accept the fact that there are men who simply enjoy the company of men. When two men go out together, entertain together, or even live together, there is no reason to assume they sleep together. No woman seems to object to the overt congeniality that goes on in the men's locker at a gym, health spa, or country club. No one is going to point a finger at the man who

---

* *See* Question nine.

gives a friendly swat to the bare bottom of his golfing partner as he emerges from the shower.

You see how our individual interpretation determines our attitudes. We are so quick to make judgments about people when judgments are not necessary. Who a man chooses for his friends and companions is entirely up to him. This is a freedom granted to all.

3. *An abrupt change in your ex-husband's living style, manner of dress, choice of occupation*

One of the few good things about divorce is that you do have the opportunity to change your pattern or style of living. All of us get into ruts, bogged down by commitments and frightened by predictable futures. Dreams are not limited to women. Even the happiest of married men has been known to fantasize chucking it all for a nomadic life in the Caribbean.

Women think of men as totally satisfied with their role of provider, going off each morning to pit their strength and intellect against the business world. We are envious of the excitement and challenge they have in their lives. We feel sorry for ourselves, stuck at home amid the dishes and diapers with an occasional PTA meeting thrown in to sweeten the pot. Men often feel the same sense of futility.

A divorce often provides an intoxicating new sense of freedom. The husband feels the urge to step up his style of dressing. He may decide he wants a waterbed, a lucite cocktail table, and deep sideburns. His new friends could include a painter who lives on a houseboat, a sixty-year-old female novelist who writes pornographic verse, and a teacher of Zen. That doesn't mean he's a flipped out fag who should be banned from seeing his children. It is far wiser to accept his new life for what it is—his new life.

A great many ideas are changing in our attitudes toward each other. Way of living, dress, vocation, length of hair—these are no longer indicative of character. My husband knows and loves antique furniture. A great friend of mind, a woman doctor, belongs to a hunting club and spends her weekends shooting duck or pheasant. These interests and activities don't make him feminine or her masculine. Interests are interests and deserve to be accepted as such.

4. *"Terrible things I simply can't tell you"*

That is the statement of an unhappy, bitter woman

who wants to lash out and destroy. And she can. Judging anyone is risky. Judging an ex-husband is dangerous. Because the man is her ex-husband, people tend to believe her! Permanent damage can be done to the man as well as their children. Unfortunately gossip is a very big part of communication and it is kept alive by those to whom it appeals.

A wounded woman can be as dangerous as a wounded animal. Furthermore, she carries the extra impetus of a scheming brain. It is very difficult to reach a woman who has decided to destroy a man. The most successful argument I have used with such a woman is to point out what she is doing to her children. Hopefully her love for them is greater than her hatred of him.

The second appeal is more mercenary than humanitarian. If a man is sufficiently blasphemed that he loses his job, how will she collect child support? What is to keep him from leaving the state or even the country? Is any revenge ever really worth the time and trouble it takes to inflict? Doesn't an unfair judgment come back upon the judge with a force and violence that is devastating to behold? Think about it.

One of the questions I asked on the eight-page questionnaire I sent to divorced women over the country was, "In your heart what do you honestly feel caused your divorce?" The most unusual and yet one of the most heartbreaking replies I received was from a woman on the East Coast. She said she came home from work two or three separate times and found her husband dressed up in her clothes. She said she was terribly upset and afraid he was crazy. She never mentioned this in her divorce proceedings in exchange for his promise not to see their two small children after the divorce.

She wrote a postscript on the back of the questionnaire to the effect that she was sorry now she had handled the situation in that manner. The husband moved out of the state, remarried, and had become a very responsible and successful businessman. She said he sent money regularly but she wished he could do more by becoming a real father to her children. She was finding it more and more difficult to answer their questions about their father and she was dreading the future.

Who knows what prompted this man to try on his wife's clothes. Perhaps he was not the success in business he wished to be and apprehension of failure in his role of provider made him react in this unusual way. Obviously the man did straighten out his thinking. Had his first wife been more concerned about him as a human being and less worried about the reaction of "society" she would not have a dedicated father for her children and perhaps a husband for herself.

CONCLUSION:

Even if her husband is a confirmed homosexual, I am not sure a woman should seek modification of visiting rights until she seeks advice and counsel from a knowledgeable professional source. To instigate legal proceedings without such advice could be damaging to all concerned. Because after all, the only, only, concern here is for the children. Any adult should be free to conduct his or her life according to individual preferences. The only irrevocable rule is that he or she bring harm to no one else.

You cannot keep your children hermetically sealed from the real world. You can equip them with standards and values for choosing their own way of life. Since you are the parent who spends the most time with the children, make it time well spent. Don't forget that your mode of living has the greatest effect upon them. You are the parent they see the majority of the time. What you do, how you react, what you accomplish, what you consider the essentials—all add to your children's development and their success for building a happy, rewarding life. Make your statement by the life you lead rather than pointing a finger at the life *he* leads.

I Am in Love with a Man My Children Do Not Like. What Should I Do?

If you are not contemplating marriage with this man, this is not such a pressing problem. Certainly you should continue to see him. If you are contemplating marriage, the problems should be resolved before the marriage. It is a demonstrated truth that marriage never solves existing problems. It generally creates a whole new batch. To help you meet this problem here are some positive steps to take.

Step One: List the Grievances

Make it clear to the children that you want to discuss the problem with them privately. Caution them not to discuss it with anyone else. Most particularly tell them not to mention the conversation to the man in question.

Ask the children to make a list of their grievances against the man. When you go over the list with them, keep an open mind. They may have some enlightening observations. Then view each grievance with these facts in mind:

a. Their loyalty to their father
b. Their natural competitiveness with a man in your life
c. Jealousy
d. Fear of change
e. Apprehension of "new rules"
f. Loss or "sharing" of inheritance

It will become apparent to you which are valid *dislikes* and which are imagined.

Step Two: His Past Life

If this man has never been married or never had children, this fact should be explained to your children. He simply may not know how to relate to children. He may be overreacting and appear juvenile. Or he may be unnaturally stiff and formal. Make the children try to see themselves as he sees them. Appeal to their sense of justice.

If your children are grown, they may know things

about this man that you don't know. If he had a previous marriage or marriages that ended in divorce, they may feel he is a poor marriage risk. If the man is from a vastly different economic level they may feel he is "taking advantage" of you. If you are older than this man, they may feel his motives need questioning. Grown children have a way of being almost too protective of parents. Again, view their grievances with the above facts in mind.

Step Three: Age of Children

If your children are very young, their dislike is probably jealousy. Children are creatures of habit and their world has already been upset once by a divorce or death. Now they might be thinking that your remarriage would be another shake-up. They probably like things the way they are.

If your children are teen-agers they may have some definite dislikes based on character. Sift through their reasons carefully. With adult teen-agers it could simply be body chemistry. They don't like him because they don't like him. In this case explain to them that you *do* like him and why. Point up his good features. Assure them that life is going to be the same or better after you're married.

If your children are grown, you must certainly give a great deal of thought to what they are saying. It is quite possible, in a lonely state, to consider marriage without looking too closely at the marriage partner. It is possible for the wrong type of man to woo you and win you. Keep in mind at all times that you, as a woman alone, *are* susceptible.

Step Four: Be Prepared

If your children are young, you do have a responsibility to them. But once they're grown, you're the one who will be left in the empty nest. If you feel this is the right man for you, then by all means go ahead. But be prepared. You will be the constant buffer between him and your children. Living together isn't necessarily going to lessen the resentment. No man wants to be running a constant popularity contest.

If you decide to go ahead with this marriage in spite of the objections of grown children, you have to be prepared for them, too. In their eagerness to find fault they could become very meddling and actually break up a marriage that might have made it on its own.

One thing you might consider before marriage is some professional counseling. Separately and as a family it might be of enormous value to "talk things out" with a qualified third person. Far better to clear the air than let it build up into a potential blow-up.

Step Five: Ground Rules

Once you do get married, start off with as many ground rules as possible. If you have young children, clearly explain to each child what is expected of him or her. It's even a good idea to put it in writing with carbon copies all around. Then:

BE CONSISTENT

BE FAIR

—AND LET HIM BE THE FATHER

A man cannot be a good stepfather unless you let him. By that I mean, back him up in his decisions, defer to his final judgment, and don't relent behind his back. Once the two of you present a united front, it's very reassuring to the children. A home with defined behavior boundaries faces fewer problems than the home with inconsistent rules.

It's not a bad idea to have ground rules with grown children. If an older son, for instance, has been handling your financial matters, it would be a good idea to now turn your affairs over to your lawyer or your banker. In his resentment of your new husband, your son's judgment could be clouded. I wouldn't immediately turn your affairs over to your new husband. A trusted family adviser is far better. This will leave your children and your new husband the room to eventually become friends, or at least be respectful of each other.

It takes a lot of living to pull a family together. The first year is the toughest. Keep telling yourself that it *is* going to work out well for everyone. A family unit is still the best living arrangement. Too many women have passed up a good man "for the sake of the children." I watched a young divorcée turn down a widower with two children because one of her girls didn't like one of his girls. It was a double tragedy because later in high school the girls became great friends. Unfortunately the widower had long since remarried. And the divorcée— is still a divorcée.

My Ex-Husband Lives with a Woman Without Benefit of Marriage. How Do I Explain This to Our Children?

I see no reason for you to explain this (or anything else he does) to your children. If they are young children, they won't truly understand. To load them down with information they are unable to grasp is an unfair responsibility to give them. As they get older and begin to ask questions, refer them to their father.

If your children are teen-agers they will already know his living arrangement without your telling them. If they specifically ask you certain questions, what they are after is your *reaction* to his living arrangement. Answer them the same way you would any adult. Do keep in mind he is their father. Don't grasp every question as a platform to air your grievances against him.

Living arrangements are changing around the world. A great many people are beginning to feel that marriage is irrelevant and are seriously considering the alternatives. Divorce is commonplace. It's quite natural that your children will question marriage. When this discussion starts, use it as a chance to make them look at the pros and cons of marriage. This is a great deal smarter than waiting until they are romantically involved before you bring it up. It's harder to be cooly rational when you are in a state of bliss.

One of the best ways to have this discussion with your teen-agers is to sit down with them and a few of their friends and have an informal round table discussion. Start by asking them to list the reasons *for* living together without marriage. Then ask them to list the reasons *against*. After they have made their lists, discuss it point by point. Believe me, you'll learn a lot.

I've done this with several groups of teen-agers and here are the highlights of some of these discussions:

For Living Together Without Marriage:

1. *You can split at will*

   Most young people today are very jealous of their freedom and tend to shy away from things that smack of regimentation. Marriage used to be the major escape from parental control. Now the escape options are many. Divorce being as common as it is, nearly every young person knows it intimately through his own life—or through the experiences of a close friend. And divorce is what you must go through when you split—if you're married.

2. *You can be with someone body and mind without a permanent commitment*

   To sleep with someone you care about, openly, at will, is a highly electric notion. Sex is certainly a big attraction, but not as an isolated act. The physical nearness, the touching and the talking, all add to the total scene. To be able to do all this without a marriage contract makes it even more titillating. When it's over—it's over.

3. *You can find out if you like marriage before you marry*

   Living together certainly does give two people a chance to see each other in close-up. It's a way for them to observe each other under pressure, and pleasure, and decide if, indeed, they are made for each other. Some young people are not sure they want to ever get married and so this does seem like a sensible way to find out. If the going gets bumpy—bye, bye.

4. *You are really on your toes*

   It's no secret that a lot of women and men slack-off in marriage. They just don't try as hard to please or to be pleasing. Physical appearance doesn't mean as much, manners are not a necessity and selfishness takes over. In an unmarried state you try harder. Some young people feel they would continue to try harder if they weren't bound together legally. You are there because you want to be—not *have* to be.

5. *You have all of the good and none of the bad*

   In other words, you have no obligation to anyone or anything if the living arrangement isn't exactly what you want, the way you want it. No responsibility to behave any way except the way you feel. Freedom to come and go at will. No pressure, no commitment, no responsibility. Nirvana.

AGAINST LIVING TOGETHER WITHOUT MARRIAGE:

1. *You might have children*

   A child is a permanent souvenir of a liaison. And a child becomes someone's responsibility. So immediately commitments would have to be made. The mother of the child must care for it and the father provide for it. If one decides to leave, the other must assume the responsibilities. Of course, the court would try to make the father pay were he to leave, but it's a long hard battle.

   If a couple decided to stay together with the child without being married, they face the problem of later telling the child. Most young women I've talked to say they would not want children unless they were married. So the arrival of a child forces an entirely new set of circumstances. Ultimately it is the woman and the child who suffer if the unit dissolves.

2. *You hurt your family*

   In spite of the surface air of abandon, most young people do not want to hurt their parents. Even those young people who march off dry-eyed have a twinge of conscience now and again. The accompanying hassle between parent and child mars the "beauty" of the new relationship. The couple find themselves always looking over their shoulders and wondering "what people think."

   The nomadic couple must come to grips with the world and themselves "sometime." If they have completely severed ties with their parents, it closes an avenue of help. Even the families who "try to understand" can't help censuring those who run off without adequate means or a way to support themselves.

3. *You could blow your mind*

   Most girls feel it is the woman who carries the psychological load in living together. She worries the most about what they've done and what will happen if she's left alone. She also cares the most about what people are saying. Girls feel they put the greatest effort into the relationship, try the hardest, and have the most to lose.

   Jealousy is also a big factor and works both ways.

With no formal commitment each is afraid the other will find someone new. Every side glance or late arrival causes a blow-up and destroys any relationship. When it's over, you have emotional scars that could last a lifetime.

If either the boy or the girl begins to dwell on the opportunities they missed by leaving home, the "idyllic" relationship becomes a jail. When the hard facts of making one's way in the world are at last realized, the reasons for leaving home are pale in comparison to the reasons once given for staying. Awakening to the fact that you can't "go home" very possibly *could* blow your mind.

4. *You don't pay a high enough price*
Interestingly enough it is the boys who say the girls make it too easy. Why should they ever get married when there are so many female roommates available. If two people go into a relationship demanding nothing of each other—they often get nothing. Today's young woman has eliminated the element of the chase. Her new freedom tells her she doesn't have to be hard to get—that's old-fashioned. I agree more with the boys. A woman should be hard to get—not because it's a game, but because she values herself highly and doesn't care to give herself away. Her new freedom should tell her she can pick and choose because marriage or living with someone is just *one* of her options. She can pursue a career and build an exciting life on her own. Why should she put herself in a position to be deserted at will?

5. *You set a pattern*
When a woman lives with a man without marriage and then breaks up, the next man she cares about will want the same deal. Why should he have to make a commitment when the last one didn't? Girls are afraid that when it's so easy to split they might face a life of multi-relationships that have no purpose.

While I was having this discussion with a group of high school seniors one day, and I came to this question, a girl in the front row blurted out, "Boy, you can say *that* again." I asked her what she meant and she quite freely told the group about her older sister who lived with a guy and had two children. One day he decided to split so he asked his best friend if he would move in and take over for him. The sister didn't offer any objection because she knew the father of her children was going to split anyway and the new guy would at least look out for her. Two years and one more child later *he* split, but without finding a replacement. Now the sister and her three children are on welfare and trying to pull a life together.

This, to me, illustrates one of the big pluses in marriage. Marriage at least forces two people to try to solve some of their problems. When you stand toe-to-toe and hash out your gripes and grievances you are forced to grow up. Running away at the drop of a bad word or the arrival of a troubled time is not so easy.

CONCLUSION:

Marriage is in no way perfect. But after all the arguments are presented, I still believe it is the best living arrangement for a man and woman and most certainly for children. By conducting this sort of open, free discussion you allow your children to reach their own conclusions. Continually preaching at them is no answer. They will resent it and do what they want to do anyway. To help you start a group discussion with your children, here is an outline to use.

Reference Outline for Discussion
Two young people living together.

Pro:
1. Can be terminated at will
2. Satisfies the sexual needs without permanent involvement
3. See if you're made for each other. Test marriage
4. Keeps you on your toes
5. Only good without the bad

Con:
1. Pregnancy
2. Family and society
3. Mentally disturbing to woman—and man
4. Price isn't high enough. Too easy to split
5. Next guy wants same deal. Sets pattern

I Want My Ex-Husband Back. How Can I Get Him?

The answer to this question depends upon the conditions leading to the divorce, who actually wanted the divorce, how long you've been divorced, and whether either of you has remarried. Read through all these descriptions and find the one that most nearly describes the marriage you had with your former husband, and the consequent divorce. Be objective about the two of you. Don't just remember the good times.

CONDITIONS:

1. *Slowly disintegrating*

   There is a certain security in the worst of marriages. There is companionship of sorts, there is habit, there is identity. If you understand these feelings for what they are, you are able to look with deeper perspective at your own emotions.

   If your marriage was a slowly disintegrating one, without many moments of real happiness, what you are missing is the state of marriage and not the man. Wanting to put back a marriage based only on these things is a form of suicide. That may sound like a harsh word. It isn't. You are saying to yourself that you will trade your life for a name, a male roommate, and a set of rules and responsibilities.

2. *Cruelty*

   If your marriage was based on cruel behavior there must be something in your makeup that causes you to miss this bad treatment. The human body can learn to love pain, if pain is all that is presented to love.

   What do I mean by cruel behavior? If your husband abused you physically, drank excessively, disappeared regularly, didn't contribute to the support of the family or taunted you with other women—any of these would constitute cruel behavior. What a man does in one marriage situation, he will more than likely repeat in another marriage situation—especially with the same woman.

Before you consider putting yourself through torture and torment again, try to find out what it is within you that seeks this type of punishment. A woman, married for twenty-three years, came to a lawyer friend of mine for a divorce. She said her husband had been beating her all twenty-three years but she was finally finished with him and the marriage. The lawyer referred her to a psychiatrist for consultation before he would accept the case. The woman objected at first but the lawyer insisted. "Look" he said to her, "aren't you at all curious *why* you put up with this treatment for twenty-three years?"

After the woman's second visit to the psychiatrist the doctor called the lawyer and told him the woman and her husband were a casebook example of perfectly meshed neuroses. He is a sadist; she, a masochist. He recommended the divorce proceedings begin as the woman had agreed to continued medical treatment. Had the lawyer not intervened and simply gotten the woman her divorce, she undoubtedly would have continued to seek and expect bad treatment, not only from men, but in her work, her friendships, and in every facet of living.

3. *Peaks and valleys*

Some marriages are built solely on the excitement of fighting-to-make-up-to-fight again. A marriage like this is constantly in trouble. The need to vent hostilities on a partner is indicative of a lack of respect for that partner as a separate human being. Certainly any marriage has its moments of turmoil, but these moments should be genuine constructive disagreements. You should *know* the difference. If your marriage was one of great peaks and valleys, you are remembering the ups and erasing the downs.

If, however, you feel that the good times outweighed the bad and are willing to settle for half, know in advance what you are "going back to"—only worse. It is almost impossible to build a meaningful lasting relationship based on turmoil.

4. *A giant blowup*

If your marriage was perking along as well as most, but broke up over one great big problem, then perhaps you can put it back together. But generally

71

speaking, that one "irreconcilable difference" is merely a scapegoat. One or the other of you "wanted out" and the situation gave you the key.

To illustrate, let's say a husband and wife had a giant fight and the wife said something so totally devastating to the husband that he struck her. He had never hit her before and would never do such a thing under normal conditions. But the wife screamed, "That's cause for divorce" and tells him to leave forever. I can't help but feel that a good solid marriage could take one such singular blow without cracking apart.

Be sure your one giant blowup was just that and not simply the escape hatch for the partner who wanted out. You can tell the difference by reading these descriptions of marriages and seeing if perhaps your "blowup" was simply indicative of some deeper trouble.

5. Infidelity

Real or imagined, infidelity is always a sure way to obtain a divorce. The aggrieved party has a socially accepted reason to cry, "Out. . . . You have defiled the marriage!" There are, however, all types and styles of infidelity—some serious, some not so serious.

The most common type of infidelity is the traveling business man who engages in an occasional peccadillo when the timing, geography, and willing partner all conspire to "lead him astray" for the night. He truly is not unhappy in his marriage; he doesn't want a divorce; and, when pressed, he doesn't even remember the girl's name!

If this is the type of man you divorced and he was a good husband and father in all other ways, perhaps you can put your marriage back together. If you won't always be suspicious and nagging, he may even outgrow this behavior. Maybe. Then again, he may not want to come back now that he has had total freedom.

If your husband had a torrid affair with one woman, this is serious infidelity. Obviously your divorce left him with the freedom to marry her. If he didn't and you want him back, be sure you have first given yourself every opportunity to test your feelings for him. It's very damaging to a woman's sense of worth when her husband finds someone else.

However, it is possible for a married man to have a

love affair with another woman and then decide it is still his wife whom he wants and whom he genuinely loves. If your ex-husband has decided he made "a terrible mistake" and has suggested he would like to come home, and you want him, tell him so. It could be that with your understanding attitude and his newly revived love of you, your remarriage could become a lasting and happy one.

Whatever you do, don't go after your ex-husband if he has not shown any interest in you or mentioned that his love affair is over. Perhaps he has not married the woman for reasons that have nothing at all to do with you. Let him be and concentrate on your own life.

If it was your infidelity that caused the divorce, getting your ex-husband back might be quite difficult—and not what you want at all. A very glamorous woman in Dallas is about to be married again after being a divorcée for three years. Her first husband was a fiery Latin and his amorous attentions to other women were flagrant. His love trysts filled his calendar to overflowing. Many of us wondered why this most attractive woman put up with this.

Her friends were startled one day to read that her husband was suing for divorce! After the announcement he called all their mutual friends to say he was the cuckold husband. He said she had taken a lover and disgraced him forever. He made a great deal of commotion and did obtain a divorce. The wife later confided to her friends that she had had one affair that consisted of two lunches and one dinner with the same man. She had gone to bed with the man, she said, because she wanted to be loved. Her conduct, unlike her husband's, had been terribly discreet. But when the husband found out he raised all kinds of hell, public and private.

The following three years this woman suffered terribly from self-incriminations and the hostility of her ex-husband. She felt worthless and totally ashamed of her behavior. Her friends tried to tell her that what she did was perfectly natural and that she was not the villain at all. She finally began to date and eventually met a fabulous man who fell in love with her. When it became obvious to the ex-husband that she cared about this man also, he tried to talk her into remarrying him again. Fortunately she had outgrown her ex-husband to the point where his feelings for her, or torture of her, no longer mattered at all. She could look at him for what he was—and at herself for what she was.

Imagined infidelity is almost as devastating as real infidelity. The wife who is constantly checking for lipstick on her husband's collar. The husband who comes home at odd hours to see if his wife is alone. This kind of behavior can drive a spouse crazy. The most advanced case of infidelity hallucination I ever heard about was the husband who accused his wife of having a lover because he found the shower curtain was damp when he came home for lunch.

Suspicious people are sick people. If your husband was constantly questioning you about men or you were nagging him about women, one or the other of you needs help. A good marriage should allow for human behavior. A wife should be able to have lunch with a man friend, openly and honestly. A husband should be able to have lunch with a woman friend, openly and honestly. Pointing fingers and calling names indicates that the marriage is in trouble. The marriage is in trouble because the partners are in trouble.

6. *Immaturity*

Immaturity is defined by *Webster's New World Dictionary* as: "not mature, not completely grown or developed; not ripe, not finished or perfected; incomplete." Very few human beings are complete, but the adult attitude is to keep trying, to keep growing. In marriage the mature attitude is concern for each other, awareness of each other's needs, the desire to help each other. Immaturity in one partner allows for none of this.

An immature husband is unable to relate to his wife in any adult way. Many men are able to be successful in business from nine to five and then come home and turn into selfish little boys. Many women can be good mothers then pout and stamp their feet at their husbands. If your marriage fell apart because one or the other of you couldn't grow up, remarriage would be impossible.

Immaturity also causes jealousy, which can erupt in many forms. Perhaps he was jealous of your ability to get along with people, or you were jealous of his work. He could have been jealous of his mother. Jealousy is negative energy. And negative energy destroys.

Many, many marriages have dissolved due to the sexual unawareness of one of the partners. If a man is immature he considers only his gratification and has little feeling for the needs of his wife. An immature wife will hold herself aloof from her husband and only let him touch her when she wants something. Neither of these people are "complete" enough for marriage.

It's not unusual for an immature person to marry many times. Part of their immaturity is to split when they can't have their way. An immature person lacks self-esteem. Without self-esteem they don't have the confidence to work out problems. It's useless also to give in to an immature person. When one is incapable of giving, one is also incapable of receiving, at least with any understanding and graciousness. If immaturity was why your marriage dissolved, a lot of growing up is needed in order to reconstruct it.

Now that you have read through these six basic conditions that cause divorce and have identified your marriage, ask yourself these questions:

WHO WANTED THE DIVORCE?

1. If he wanted the divorce, list all the reasons he gave. Now list all the reasons he didn't give but you know were factors. Look at this list. Ask yourself these questions about each reason:
   a. Will my changing correct the fault?
   b. Should I change to correct the fault?
   c. What will happen to me as a person if I change to correct the fault?
   Your answer should indicate whether you are the cause of his unhappiness with the marriage. Chances are, you're not.
2. If you asked for a divorce, list all the reasons you gave. Now list all the secret reasons you didn't give. Ask yourself these questions about each reason:
   a. Will his changing correct the problem?
   b. Is he able to change if he wants to?
   c. Is it his desire to change?
   This is a very important test. Everyone should be given

75

a second and even a third chance to change—if it's coupled with a strong desire and motivation to do so. On the other hand no one should be forced to change simply to fit in with someone else's notion of how they should behave. You have to be able to be yourself in marriage—as well as in life!

How Long Have You Been Divorced?

This is an important factor in determining whether you sincerely do want your husband back. If you are just recently divorced, give yourself a full year's wait. Emotionally you are still in no frame of mind to know what you want. If you've been divorced over a year and still feel you want him back, take this test. Make a list of what you've done this past year. It should include:

1. Any jobs you've had
2. Serious suitors
3. Trouble or satisfaction with your children
4. Change in living pattern
5. Condition of your social and community life

Examine the list. You should have had a job, interesting men in your life, both good and bad times with your children, a change in your living pattern, and a new social and community life. If you haven't met any new men you are bored, full of self-doubts, and lonely. If you have lost contact or control of your children you are selfish, introverted, and feeling sorry for yourself. If you are still trying to lead the exact same life you did, you are fooling yourself. If you don't have new friends and activity in the community you are living in a shell, not trying to build a new life for yourself, and ignoring a great big wonderful world out there. No wonder you want your ex-husband back. But on the other hand—I can see why he left!

You must be able to see what we are attempting to do here together. I'm forcing you to look at you. Because only then can you judge accurately why you want your ex-husband back. Here is one last test to take.

Remarriage:

1. If he has remarried and you are single, it is jealousy that is behind your desire to have him back. You

want him because someone else has him and you think you are missing something. Give up the idea. His remarriage should be news enough of his feelings for you. If he says otherwise it is doubtful he means it. He probably doesn't want to see *you* married again.

2. If you are remarried and your ex-husband is single, you must have made a bad second marriage. Or perhaps your first husband knows you so well that he is able still to upset you. Taunting you in your second marriage may just be a game with him. You owe your new husband the decency not to see your ex-husband alone. You must let go of the past if the future is to have a meaning. If you must communicate with your ex-husband, do so by mail.

3. If you are both remarried and are contemplating simultaneous divorces, I can only suggest you seek some professional counseling. The multiple heartache involved here is staggering. There are absolutely no guarantees that you can make any marriage work. Better to forget the whole thing and concentrate on the marriage you have.

4. If neither of you has remarried, and you feel you sincerely want to try it again, then make a list of the reasons why. Force yourself to put down on paper *all* the thoughts going through your head. It isn't enough to simply say you love him. You said that before, remember? List all the good things about him, his habits, his strong points, his weak points, his physical makeup. Your list should include his financial capability because that should be a consideration. Hopefully remarriage will improve both your positions. The children should be a factor. Your individual growth is certainly a reason. Keep searching until they are all down on that piece of paper. You still want to try? Okay.

How to Go About It:

Before you delve into this campaign, promise to be *honest* with yourself, and promise that you won't go back with him if there are any unresolved doubts in your head. This is the time to find out, not after you've made another mistake.

STEP I: *Don't tell anyone what you are doing*

Don't ask for help or give progress reports. Keep your private life private.

STEP II: *Make an overture*

Call him at his place of work or at home and ask to meet him somewhere for cocktails or dinner. No lunch—it's not time enough. Not at your home—especially if it's the one you shared.

STEP III: *Be honest*

When he asks why the call, tell him that you want to talk to him. That's all. Don't have any made-up excuses about the children, your family, finances—just say you want to see him to talk to him.

STEP IV: *Don't ask him to come back*

This is letting yourself in for a big punch. It's too sudden and too final. Tell him you miss him. Be specific. You made a list of why you wanted him, now work some of those good things into the conversation.

STEP V: *Don't flirt*

All the phony social games of the first-time-a-round are no good here. Solid conversation and communication is what is called for.

STEP VI: *Take a clue*

If he chain smokes, looks at his watch every five minutes, and seems not to be listening—he isn't. Give him every opportunity to partici-pate, but if he simply isn't buying, turn your cheek and make a speedy exit. No pleas, no protestation, no tears. For God's sake hang on to yourself! If, on the other hand, he's listening, pleased, and genuinely glad to see you, bore in a little harder.

STEP VII: *Tell him you'd like to see more of him*

No pacts, no promises, no problems. The next move has to be his. Unless he is totally dense he'll start picking the times and places.

STEP VIII: *Set some ground rules*

If you have children *don't* involve them. You don't know what's going to become of this so let them be. They've been through enough al-ready. The same goes for family and friends.

STEP IX: *Take your time*

Even if you end up in bed on your first date,

don't rush out and get married. You've got time to be sure—so be sure.

STEP X: *Continue with your life*

Don't quit your job, turn down social engagements, or shirk your responsibilities. Keep going. This may or may not work but *your* life should move forward. If you do in fact decide to remarry, continue working on your life. Getting married is not giving up.

My approach to this problem may seem like the long way around to the answer to your original question. What I am trying to avoid for you is a situation that would cost you in self-respect, self-confidence, and self-love. No man and no marriage is worth self-hate.

As a woman alone you do, in rough times, wish for deliverance. This wish can take the form of your ex-husband. After all, the two of you did begin in an atmosphere of excitement, romantic dates, hushed whispers, stolen moments. It wasn't all bad. Surely you do remember the good. What you are suppressing is how this marriage evolved. Were you to go back exactly as you were, you would revolve in the old rut like a phonograph needle on a scratched record.

You can't go back in life because the very concept of "going back" is contrary to nature. Mankind is best when striving. To turn back out of fear, insecurity, or self-distrust is admitting defeat. The only possible way for you and your ex-husband to make a marriage is to come together as two people who have grown in many ways and who both want to build a *new* and better life.

Your life, at the moment, is what should concern you. You are in charge and you can have a great life without your ex-husband.

My Fiancé Shows an Unnecessary Amount of Affection to My Eighteen-Year-Old Daughter. What Should I Do?

This situation is such a potential powder keg that I strongly urge you to do nothing and say nothing until you read my entire answer. I further urge you to then seek other help if a question still exists in your mind. What is at stake here is not only your future happiness with this man but your future relationship with your daughter.

The first step is to define the problem. This you do by asking yourself a series of questions.

1. Are you newly divorced or recently widowed?
2. Is this man your first major affair since your divorce or your husband's death?
3. Are you quite certain *he* is looking forward to marrying you?
4. Do you still feel in competition with the women in his life?
5. Do you have any qualms about what he's doing when he's not with you?

The purpose of these questions is to determine your mental attitude toward this man. If you are a newly divorced or widowed woman you shouldn't be making judgments of other people's emotions. Physically and mentally you are just not up to it. Either ordeal leaves you with all nerve endings dangling. You have a tendency to fantasize. Jealousy becomes one of your major emotions. You constantly feel threatened, insecure, inadequate. Judgment is not your strong point.

It would be quite simple at this time to mistake a genuine liking of your daughter on the part of your fiancé, for a lecherous urge. He may be trying very hard to like your children for your sake. He may have come from a boisterous and tactile family and think nothing of hugging and kissing all the members of the family. What you think "unnatural" he may label "usual."

If you have any doubts about this man's willingness to marry you, these doubts could be clouding your thinking. If you are pressing for this marriage this could be a bit of your guilt or feeling of inadequacy rising to the surface. No woman likes to feel she's predatory. This could be a way of soothing your conscience. "He doesn't want me; he wants my daughter." A fact could be that you're not sure he wants you at all—with or without a daughter.

If you tend to be a jealous woman your relationships with all men are going to be in trouble. Jealousy makes us consider all women potential foes. Jealousy makes us see a man's occupation not as his work but as an excuse to spend time away from home. Jealousy makes us feel totally cuckold most of the time. We are being plotted against, talked about, and avoided. Then what happens? Because this jealousy makes us such impossible shrews, all the fears come true.

I hope you are beginning to see why it's so important not to speak out in hurt and anger. Until you are genuinely sure you have an issue, be still. Continue questioning yourself.

The next set of questions concern your daughter:

1. Is your daughter causing any part of this problem?
2. Is she initiating incidents for your benefit?
3. Could this be a scheme on her part to break up your relationship and cause you hurt and embarrassment?
4. Do you see your daughter as a daughter—or another woman?

Problems with living are not unique to adults. Your daughter has had her adjustments to make. Perhaps she is transferring her feelings for her absent father to this man. It could be that she genuinely cares for him and is more demonstrative than you. If you are divorced she could feel rejected by her father and be reaching out to this man for her love and reassurance.

Or her actions could genuinely be termed "bitchy." She's a female *and* a daughter. She could be vying for this man's affection without his realizing what she is up to. If this is the case she will tire of the game when she realizes you aren't going to play. By saying nothing you have robbed her of her incentive. Making a scene would dignify a childish attitude and lower you in everyone's eyes.

Try always to regard your daughter as your daughter. Be glad for her successes and offer your comfort when she fails. Don't compete with her, guide her. She has to find her way with this man as surely as you do. Eventually she will settle into a role that feels more natural for all concerned. She will be watching you closely, so show no emotion at her antics.

The next set of questions concerns your fiancé:

1. Could his interest be described as "parental"?
2. Is he showing his affection with small gifts or is he being overtly physical?
3. Could his actions be described as "erotic"?
4. If her natural father treated her the same way would it be called "erotic" or "parental" behavior?

Your fiancé's affectionate attitude toward your daughter might well be his definition of how a father should act. Perhaps he has never had a daughter and is overacting the part. He may feel in competition with her natural father and is trying to win her over. Again, as your relationship continues, all members of the group should settle into their rightful roles.

If, after all these questions, you can in all honesty say you think your fiancé's overtures toward your daughter are erotic, you will have to reach some conclusion as to what to do. The first major decision should be to speak to him or to her. Which one will depend largely on your relationship with your daughter. If the two of you are close and exchange confidences, I advise you to start with her.

The best approach is to ask her, when you're alone, what she truly thinks about your fiancé. It is always flattering to have your opinion asked and your daughter may have been waiting for just such an opportunity to talk to you. She should have some definite opinions and from these you can judge how far to press the conversation. She may say she doesn't like all the affection your fiancé showers upon her but she didn't want to say anything because she didn't want to hurt anyone's feelings. If this is the case, urge her to speak to your fiancé. The fewer people that are involved the better. Suggest she simply tell him how much she cares about him, but she's not a demonstrative person and she doesn't like the physical contact. He should certainly get the picture from a statement like that.

If, on the other hand, your daughter bristles and acts secretive when the fiancé is mentioned, I feel you have every right to press forward with the questioning. Don't show anger or jealousy, just a keen desire to know what she feels. If you have been close in the past it will be hard for her to refrain from telling you things now.

If you and your daughter have not been close in the past years and you feel there is nothing to be gained by conversation with her along these lines, then it's up to you to go to your fiancé. You can start the same way with him. Ask him if he feels your daughter is a happy person. All you want is a side door to open the conversation. Once you've brought her up as a subject, he should have a great deal to say. Try to be insightful and listen to what he is saying without making judgments. You should be able to tell if his interest transcends the role of a parent. Keep in mind that she came into his life as a woman, not a crying infant. His evaluation and treatment of her is not based on years of fatherhood. It is not unusual for a man to be attracted to a younger woman—even if she is your daughter.

If, at the end of all your questioning and searching, you feel the relationship between your daughter and your fiancé is erotic, or has the potential to become so, you should make a definite decision. That decision, I feel, is to terminate your engagement. Marriage to this man is not going to solve your problems. Marriage is going to worsen the existing situation and create a potential powder keg.

Divorce, caused by just such a triangle, is not unusual. And the results are monstrous. All relationships in such an instance are destroyed. All parties can only bury their feelings and slink away in embarrassment and shame. When a court is forced to give names to situations, they loom large and ugly and remain a permanent record. Damage, done by such an exposure, reaches far beyond its actual destructive level.

CONCLUSION:

Trace your suspicions to the cause. If they are in your head alone, erase them. If they are all your daughter's misplaced fantasies, wait them out. If they are your fiancé's harmless boisterous ways, accept them. If they are grounded in a potentially dangerous situation, make a clean quick break.

In the final diagnosis you do not want to bring more trouble to your home and to your heart. When you can avoid a disaster, do so. Your first responsibility today and forever more is to yourself and your children. Following that rule you can't go far astray.

QUESTION TWENTY

I Am a New Widow in My Forties and I Need a Job. How Do I Go About Getting One?

It *is* more difficult for the woman in her forties and fifties to find work. More difficult, but not impossible. For every real barrier in the outside world, the mature woman looking for work often creates an unreal barrier within herself. The best way for you to start your job hunting is to sit down with yourself and be objective. Be objective with yourself and about yourself.

Take a piece of paper and at the top write:

ABILITY IS AGELESS

What all employers desire is a person who is reliable, hardworking, loyal, and able to exercise good judgment. None of these categories has anything to do with age, and a smart employer knows this. A smart employer also knows that as a woman over forty, statistics are in your favor.

1. Your attendance record is better than the under forty woman
2. Your turnover is lower
3. Your stability is greater
4. You have fewer family problems (i.e., small children, etc.)

You are a desirable commodity! So keep telling yourself that. You have something the world wants.

Next, on your piece of paper under "Ability Is Ageless," start listing your personal history. Category A, should be EDUCATION. Under this, list your high school and the courses you took that could be meaningful. Next, your trade school or college experience. Think back to things you did, such as work in the school cafeteria, edit school newspaper, work on rally committee. Think.

Write down category B: WORK EXPERIENCE. Under this heading list every paying job you have ever held and exactly what you did. Be specific. If you typed, put down how many words a minute. If you worked in a pet shop, what type of animals did you handle. If you worked in a store, which departments you handled.

Category C is next, VOLUNTEER ACTIVITIES. Here list your volunteer activities, neighborhood projects, church groups. Be specific in what you did. If you helped your husband in his business, list those tasks. If you kept household accounts, that's important. Any and all hobbies should also be listed. Do you swim, do needlepoint, collect bottles?

Category D is your PERSONAL DATA. Write down all the good things about yourself. Are you well-groomed, punctual, cheerful, cooperative? After you have listed all the pluses, write down the negatives. Do crowds of people bother you? Can you take constructive criticism gracefully? Is your health satisfactory to sustain you through a full working day?

Read carefully down the page and make some judgments about yourself. Do you think you would be best in a job using your head or your hands. Would you do better in a job by yourself or with groups of co-workers. What would you consider an ideal job?* Try to narrow your job category down to one or two jobs.

The next step is to prepare a resumé. This is a brief (not over two pages) summary of all the categories you have just listed. A resumé is an absolute necessity to have in job hunting, and you need several. Have professional copies made, not carbon copies. Mimeograph, multigraph, Xerox, or offset are all acceptable. Use regular typing paper for the original and type it carefully or have a friend who types well do it.

1. In the upper left-hand corner list your name, address and phone number.
2. In upper right-hand side indicate the type of job you desire.

* The Government puts out a source book called *Occupational Outlook Handbook*. Write to: U.S. Department of Labor Statistics, Washington, D.C. 20210.

3. First heading on left-hand side is WORK EXPERIENCE. In reverse order list your last three jobs, beginning with the most recent one held.
   a. State name and address of company, dates of employment, name of your supervisor and title of job you held.
   b. For each position you held tell exactly what you did: typed, took dictation, greeted customers, handled PBX equipment, bought for Junior Department, etc.

   It doesn't matter if these are paid or unpaid jobs. You may have had a highly responsible civic job that will be considered quite important.
4. The next heading is EDUCATION.
   a. List schools and dates attended. List major or principal subjects studied.
   b. List special courses taken since leaving school. Specify length of course and date completed. Include art courses, foreign language, real estate, anything you actually learned.
   c. List any on-the-job training you received.
5. VOLUNTEER ACTIVITIES comes next, if meaningful.
   a. List name and address of agencies, institutions or groups you served.
   b. Be specific and say "Museum Guide, Jade Room, 1968-1969," or "Region 3 Chairman, Heart Fund Drive, 1965."
   c. Give name, address, and title of someone familiar with what you did.
6. PERSONAL DATA is next and here describe your current status.
   a. State that you are a widow (or a divorcée) and list number of children or dependents. It isn't really necessary to list your age. Your schooling will indicate it.
   b. State geographical area in which you prefer to work and if you are free to travel.
   c. If you drive and have a driver's license, state that. Also, any other licenses you might have (real estate, hairdresser, practical nurse).
7. PERSONAL REFERENCES come last. Three names with addresses are sufficient. Pick people of good standing in the community, but be sure to clear it with them first. Choose your doctor, school principal, prominent

businessman. Don't list any of the people mentioned under WORK EXPERIENCE.*

Once you have your resumé in hand, the serious business of job hunting begins. You should plan to work at job hunting several hours a day, not just go looking after you've been to the hairdresser. Begin by alerting your family, friends, neighbors, club members that you are looking for a job, the area in which you are looking, and the kind of job you would like.

Your first job-hunting expedition should be to go to the State Training and Employment Service. They will be listed in your phone book under your State Government offices. Their services include counseling, testing, retraining, and placement. There is no charge for any of these services. In a great many areas the employment service maintains a special office for women seeking professional and managerial jobs. These offices are part of a national network and can give you information about job openings across the country.

Next stopping point should be several private employment agencies.** Look in the phone book. Be sure to visit the agencies that specialize in temporary help also. Part-time work can lead to full-time work. Every night check the Help Wanted ads in your local paper. And don't overlook your neighborhood or weekly publication. Answer the ads you feel you could fill.

Find out who the major employers are in your area and call their personnel office. Check with schools, hospitals, and government agencies. Some areas have "40-Plus Employment Clubs." The YWCA in your town could be helpful. Be alert and stay alert. It could be an article in the newspaper about a new store opening that could lead to just the job you want.

The last and most difficult part about job hunting is the personal interview. When you have made an appointment to see a prospective employer, keep these things in mind.

1. Know something about the company or person who will be interviewing you. Know what products or serv-

---

* For further help in writing a resumé, send for the pamphlet *Job Finding Techniques for the Mature Woman*. Send 30¢ to: U.S. Department of Labor, Wage and Labor Standards Administration, Women's Bureau, Washington, D.C. 20210.

** Agencies charge a fee, either paid by you or the employer. *Never* pay a fee *until* they have secured a job for you.

ices they provide. Know if they have branch offices or state-wide connections. Read their pamphlets or magazines. In other words, do some homework.

2. Be prompt. In fact be ten minutes early. Check ahead of time how long it will take you to get there and allow the longest possible time. Don't schedule interviews closer than two hours apart.

3. Dress neatly and comfortably. Don't wear a pants suit if you can possibly avoid it. If you wear glasses, wear them. Do not try to appear younger than your years. Too much makeup has the opposite effect from what it is intended to have.

4. Take with you:
   a. Two copies of your resumé; one to hand to the interviewer and one to refer to.
   b. Your Social Security number.
   c. Pencil, ball point pen, note pad.

5. If you are given a form to fill out, carefully read the *entire* form before you begin to write. Be accurate with names and dates. Consult your resumé. Write or print carefully and watch spelling and punctuation.

6. Be alert, pleasant, and business-like. Don't start spilling out your troubles to the secretary. Don't tell the interviewer how desperately you need work. Don't be nervous and fidgety. Be responsive and answer questions briefly and to the point. Have a *good* reason why you want the job. You are not asking to be in the insurance business because you like reading about car accidents!

7. It's not a good idea to ask about vacations, benefits, or salary on the first interview. But if *you* are asked what salary you would expect, you could answer by inquiring what the firm has been paying people in similar situations.

8. It is proper, at the end of the interview, to ask when you may call back. You may also ask how long they keep applications active. If the indications are that it will be some time before they need you, you might ask the interviewer if he knows of any other company who could use you.

9. Leave promptly and thank everyone who has spoken to you. Good manners are the sign of a smart woman. When you are alone, go over the interview in your head. Analyze the good and bad reactions and improve your next interview accordingly.

There *will* be "next" interviews. Maybe many, many more. But keep at it! You are a desirable person and *there is a place for you.* Make your time count! While you are looking for work during the days, arrange to take some night school courses. After a couple of interviews you can make a judgment about the things you need to do to become more employable. You will begin to know what type of jobs are available and what fields are overcrowded.

Just being out in the world is thrilling. Your job-looking should be entered into with zest and enthusiasm. Don't consider your situation in life a handicap. Working is the best way in the world to meet people, to feel worthwhile and to make a contribution. Keep going. Today may be the day someone says to you: "How soon can you report for work?"

QUESTION TWENTY-ONE

My Life Seems to Lack All the Extras— Extra Money, New Clothes, Travel Even Very Many Good Times. Is It Possible to Find These Things Without Getting Married Again?

Loss of a husband, through death or divorce, does change your standard of living. In a divorce situation an income made to stretch between two households simply means less for each. The death of a husband often leaves a woman financially unprepared. This sense of loss can be frustrating and debilitating. When you feel unable to put the "extras" back in your life your tendency is to quit trying. A second marriage then becomes a desired escape back into the more secure world of the "married woman." You are not alone in your worries; not only about the "extras," but for the essentials. Women *are* security oriented, but I *urge* you to begin right now to chip away at these feelings of inadequacy.

To answer your question, *Yes!* You can put extras back into your life, and *Yes!* You can do it without being married.

The first "extra" you mentioned was *money*. All right, let's look at money.

MONEY

The first thing we can say about it is, there never seems to be enough. Whatever you are receiving from your ex-husband or your late husband's estate, will not go on forever. The sooner you realize this, the sooner you will become realistic about work. You *should* have a job. All you know is what you've done. Who is to say what you *can* do!

Once you have taken that first job in the world of the working,* the next step is to set out on a plan of advancement. To make extra money requires extra work. While you work, keep your ears and eyes open to what is going on around you. See what other jobs are available and find out what is necessary to qualify. Ask for extra work that will not only bring in extra money but will give you extra experience. Explore the possibility of night school.

Keep alert to the possibility of going into business for yourself. I have many exciting case histories in my files of women who have successfully done this. I know of a woman who's first job as a companion to an elderly lady developed into her own business, a baby-sitting agency. Another woman worked as a waitress for three years and then opened an Omelette House. Two women in Indiana who worked in a dry-goods store decided to become partners and opened a custom-drapery business. You see, it's not the first job you take that is important, but your *attitude* toward that job. All work is honorable and ambition *is* rewarded. The saleswoman who stands sullenly behind the counter dwelling on her sore feet and sad life is not lifting her head to see what's happening. The world is happening! God isn't discriminating against you, you are! The Small Business Administration puts out hundreds of pamphlets on every phase of operating a business. They have a "Starting and Managing Series" that tells you how to start operating a small motel, small restaurant, swap shop, flower shop, music store—practically any small business you can name. Write to:

Superintendent of Documents
Government Printing Office
Washington D.C. 20402

* *See* Question Twenty.

Ask them to send you the Small Business Administration Publications list. From this list you can order the booklets that appeal to you. They even put out a pamphlet that tells how to go about borrowing money to start your business. Your only real competition in life is your self-image. If you don't think you're very capable, then you certainly will hold yourself back.

How you spend your money determines to a great extent whether you have "extra" money in your life. A budget is a must. If you have never handled money before, I strongly urge you to talk to someone who has. Keep an account book, no matter how simple. Write down what is coming in and what is going out. Check it to see where your biggest chunk goes and how you can whittle it down. Knowing what to expect each month is a great mind-reliever and allows you to plan rather than to exist by cause and effect.

After you have started keeping an account of your money, check your spending habits. Our society is full of false economies. Let me list just a few and you'll see what I mean.

1. *Convenience foods*
   Designed for the "busy homemakers," these artfully packaged, canned, and frozen goodies may save you time in preparation, true, but some are expensive beyond belief. When you consider the extra hours you work paying for them you are far better off to reorganize your cooking habits. Plan your menus a week in advance and budget your time accordingly.

2. *A car*
   Designed as a conveyance to free mankind, I find that I'm a slave to mine. Upkeep, repairs, parts, gas, insurance—it's amazing what a car does cost. If you live in an area with good public transportation you might give serious thought to selling your car. This would release a good chunk of the budget. Here's a business idea for you that could bring profit to you, the community, and the environment: operate a car-pool agency from your home. Find out the driving patterns in your area and for a small fee list people who need rides to work, children driven to school, dentist, dancing lessons, families who need older relatives taken to the doctor. Then find students who have cars and need extra money, or men driving to work in the same area—you develop the idea from here.

3. *Budget charge accounts*

Usurious at best! When you add up all your interest and carrying charges you will be shocked at how much that washing machine or new carpet actually cost you. In planning major purchases, a savings account is your best friend. Systematically putting away a little cash each month soon adds up. And it pays *you* interest. Paying cash is a habit you should court. Seeing the money change hands has a mighty sobering effect on the spend-a-holic.

4. *Your own home*

Owning a home is certainly part of the great American dream! But again it's a dream that can turn into a nightmare. With a job, your hours at home are limited. If your children are in school their interests are often away from home. If they are grown, why do you still need a home? You are faced with payments, insurance, taxes, upkeep, and that ever-present maintenance. You might considering selling your home and buying a duplex, a fourplex, or a small apartment house. This would require some research and investigation on your part. You would want a good neighborhood, a building that is eminently rentable and accessible to transportation.

The merits of this living arrangement speak for themselves. The rent you would receive from the other unit or units would make your mortgage payment in part or in full. If you have several units you should even make money. Certainly there will be headaches, disappointing tenants, and vacancies. Being a landlord isn't all gravy. But it can be done and done profitably. Start with a trip to the library. There are several books on the subject.

CLOTHES:

The second "extra" you mentioned missing from your life was new clothes. "Not having a thing to wear" is the ancient cry of the whiny wife. Most women are impulsive or special-event buyers. They wait for a very important occasion then rush into a store and try to find something that fits the event. Shopping in haste leads to unsatisfactory purchases that have no meaning in your wardrobe. You literally *can* have a closet full of clothes and nothing to wear.

To bring order to your wardrobe I suggest a healthy house

cleaning, rearranging, and updating. Take what you know you won't wear again to your local thrift shop. Have shoes cleaned and runover heels replaced. Sew on snaps and buttons. Check hemlines. Clean handbags. Then make a list of the clothes you have suitable to wear to work. See if by mixing and matching you can't come up with a couple more outfits. Make a list of your nonwork clothes. See if you have something for coming events. Checking in advance allows you to put together an outfit from your wardrobe without making an expensive trip to the dress shop.

When I was working full time in an advertising agency I planned my wardrobe each Sunday for the following week. By checking my calendar I knew which days I had to make presentations, attend client meetings, or had a lunch date. I would decide on my dress schedule, write it down on a 3x5 card, and scotch tape it to the back of my closet door. I kept all the cards and would go over them once a month to see what I had worn where. Sound like a lot of work? On the contrary, it saved me a great deal of time, and worry, and most of all, money!

If you see a decided gap in your wardrobe, like the need for a good wool suit, decide to save for it. Take into consideration the coat, shoes, and bags you now have. Try to coordinate your accessories. As a single woman with a job and a new type of social life, your clothing needs will vary. Making a definite plan helps you pull your wardrobe into shape, and gives you goals for saving money.

Probably the best step to obtaining new clothes is to learn to sew. Sewing classes are available through adult education at your local high school. Again, pick up the phone and call. If you don't own a sewing machine, rent one for a month first to see whether you and sewing are going to click. If you do, buy a secondhand machine. Don't get pulled into buying a new deluxe machine on the installment plan! A sewing machine is like a stove; new design, gimmicks, attachments, and time-savers are unnecessary. If the needle goes up and down, you can make a dress.

Learning to sew allows you to have the kind of garments you want rather than being forced into buying budget items that don't stand up well. Watch the fashion magazines and *Women's Wear Daily* to see what's new. (No, don't buy them! Read them at the library on your lunch hour). Spend some time walking through fabric stores. Ask where the remnants are. There are great bargains in fabulous goods if you watch for them. Sewing is very creative as well as economical. You will feel a real sense of accomplishment when you slip into that floor-length hostess skirt. Why spend days drooling in front of the window of the boutique around the corner from your office when you can make that creation yourself.

TRAVEL:

If travel is the third missing extra on your list, define on paper what it is you feel you are missing. Is it the eight-day-seven-night Fiesta Week in Mexico advertised in the Sunday paper? Is it that all your life you have wanted to see the Isle of Capri? Or is it simply a nagging within you that says, "I never get to go anyplace!"

If your travel desire is in either of the first two categories, then there is no reason why you can't start planning to go. If it's in the latter, you are indulging in self-pity again and that's not an emotion that will ever get you anywhere!

Travel is becoming less and less a luxury reserved for the very rich. Group charters, vacation packages, reduced fares all make travel attractive and available to anyone willing to make the effort. Advance planning, however, is a must.

The first step is to determine exactly where you do want to go. Let's say your choice is the Costa del Sol in Spain. Go into a travel agency and tell one of the agents you are planning to take a trip next year to Spain and you want some information on the Costa del Sol. The agent will give you many colored folders and various charges of air fare. Take them home and locate your destination in the atlas. Just looking at the map of Spain is exciting. Look up the little towns and villages in the encyclopedia and read about them. You might even ask your neighborhood librarian for some books on the area. I find librarians enormously helpful, well-informed people. You might write to the mayor of one of the Spanish towns. It only costs about twenty-five cents and it could reward your handsomely.

Part of your travel research should be to find out the best time to visit. The peak of the good weather is not necessarily the best or most rewarding time. Celebrations local to the area are often well worth planning around. A change of climate could be part of the attraction.

The next step is picking a date. Naturally it will have to coincide with your vacation. But make it far enough in advance to allow time for getting the money together. From your research you should have a fairly realistic idea of what the trip will cost. Divide the cost by the number of paychecks you will receive before departure and see how much you will have to put away out of each. If it's a staggering amount, put the trip over to the next year and divide the payments in half. This will test your desire (and determination) to go. Isn't it better to have a dream with a goal than a dream without a goal?

Step three is to open a savings account to hold your "trip money." Deposit the desired amount every payday. There is nothing wrong with telling your family what you're doing. Perhaps birthday and Christmas presents will become a donation to the fund. People love to help someone along who has a definite project with a specific goal.

Don't be hesitant to plan such a trip by yourself. You'll have a far better time than if you dragged a girlfriend along. Traveling is a marvelous way to meet people and you won't be alone for long. The more you travel the better you become at it. You'll learn all the economic shortcuts of the seasoned traveler. As in most ventures, your success will be in direct proportion to the amount of time spent and the honesty of your desire.

Another possibility to explore is a working vacation in England. If you have secretarial skills you can replace a British secretary while she takes her vacation. Of course you'll have to type tyre (tire), gaol (jail), programme, kilometre, endeavour, and other specialities of the land. But what do you care? Just think, you'll be able to visit nearby Scotland for the weekend!

Salary in England would be considerably less, but you would receive free medical care. Suits, pants suits, skirts, and sweaters would be your wardrobe. Night time is more dressy than here and long dresses are often worn to restaurants and the theater. You would probably share an apartment with at least one other girl. However, food is enormously reasonable and you would eat well.

The following employment agencies specialize in summer jobs in London:

1. Miss Liberty, Inc.
   705 Soneleigh Road
   Baltimore MD 21212
   (Representative conducts interviews in major American cities.)
2. Mayfair, Ltd.
   123 Montgomery Street
   San Francisco CA 94104

3. Manpower, Inc.
   820 N. Plankinton Avenue
   Milwaukee, Wisconsin 53202
   Attn: Eileen Nock, Coordinator
        Work-Travel Program.

If you are between the ages of twenty-one and fifty, can type and take shorthand, write to one of these agencies. They will tell you what you need besides a work permit and a round-trip ticket. If you speak French, Italian, Spanish, or German you might investigate the same sort of summer work plan in other countries. To work and live in a country is possibly the best way to know a country and its people.

If you did a great deal of traveling while you were married you might explore the possibility of working for a travel agency. Connected with a travel bureau, you receive drastic cuts in fares. You might look into becoming a tour guide. There are several companies that specialize in study tours for teen-agers. This might appeal to you. I have a very close friend in Los Angeles who wanted to take her children to Europe, but her funds were low. To pay her way and that of her two boys she organized a group of teenagers with herself as guide. Since she did the work of finding the teens, the travel bureau she dealt with paid the extra three fares.

GOOD TIMES:

There is absolutely no reason for the final "extra"—very many good times—to be missing from your life. First, what do you consider a good time? Define your idea of a good time and then look at it closely. Outside of ballroom dancing, tennis, and lovemaking there are very few things you can't do on your own.

If your idea of a perfect evening is a gourmet dinner, ask three women friends if they would like to participate. Divide up the menu, set a date, and invite four men. (Or three married couples and a date for yourself). You determine your life-style by how you set the pace. It isn't a lack of money that stops most women but a lack of initiative. Style can *most certainly* be learned.

I have a friend who counsels at our local junior college in the Continuing Education for Women program. She has repeatedly told me one of the hardest jobs she faces is convincing divorced and widowed women that *they* can set the standards for the life they want to live. There is absolutely no reason you have to continue doing things the way you have always done them. He's gone and you're *here*. Do things the way *you* would like to do them.

A widow of fifty-five was taking watercolor painting lessons from a teacher in Los Angeles. It was something she had *always* wanted to do. She enjoyed them so thoroughly she added basic figure drawing and still-life sketching lessons to her schedule. Three nights a week she took creative stitchery and once a month a class in decoupage. When I met her she had just been notified that her inherited income was going to be cut drastically. She was terribly upset at the prospect of giving up all her lessons. She had also been advised that she must sell her large home immediately and move into an apartment, conserving her modest funds as best she could.

I suggested to the woman that she do nothing until she sat down with herself and *decided* what way of life she would most enjoy. This idea of "picking" a way of life was quite foreign to her. She argued that she must certainly do what her advisers suggested. I asked her to please reconsider as this was a turning point in her life. Once the house was sold and the lessons cancelled, she would be a frightened, restricted woman relegated to counting pennies and filling lonely hours.

I didn't see her again for two years, and I probably would never have seen her again except for a chance visit from an artist friend of mine. Our old coastal villages in northern California, once thriving seaports in the days of the lumber schooners, are enjoying a rebirth as artists colonies. Weathered Victorian houses blossoming in new coats of paint are now art galleries, craft centers, and gourmet restaurants. My visiting friend insisted on a drive north and a tour of the Coast. So we went.

Presiding over a glorious collection of tiny slate-gray houses in the second town we visited was the widow lady from Los Angeles! Greeting us in a hand-loomed floor-length skirt, knitted shawl, and hammered tin earrings, she insisted we be her guests for tea. Each one of the tiny houses, she explained, had originally been built as guest cabins for the seafaring men of eighty years ago. The main house had belonged to a lumber baron and was now her home, an inn and a fine restaurant with a breathtaking view of the rugged coastline.

Over tea our widow hostess told us she had sold her large home and with one-third of the money bought this collection of dwellings, all in crying need of repair. With another one-third of the money she remodeled the big house first and

97

opened the inn and the restaurant. The last one-third of the money she put in a savings account, 'just in case," where it has remained intact. The tiny houses she rented one by one to other artists and craftsmen to use as studios and galleries. The entire colony was flourishing. Perhaps they are all not making fortunes, but they pay the rent. And the widow is surrounded by the activity she loved. Her security is in her own endeavor. "I'm not afraid anymore," she said, "because the worst thing that could possibly have happened to me, I avoided. Everything that happens here, I welcome."

Be honest with yourself. Is it good times you're missing or eligible men? If it's the good times, initiate them yourself. Don't sit home waiting to be rescued like a drowning sailor on a rock. Go to a football game if that's what you like. Buy a ticket to the theater to see that new play, if *that's* what you like. I met a terrific man in a theater in New York where I had gone *all alone* to see a play that especially appealed to me. We had late supper together after the show and many months of delightful dinners whenever he happened to be in California. My New York friends were dumbfounded at my good fortune and claimed they had *never* thought of meeting anyone that way. Why not? He was as happy to meet me as I was to meet him.

Good times and a good life *are* quite possible for you. But you have to work at creating them the way you work at your job. Plan your evenings and weekends. Don't just do whatever comes up. More times than not, what comes up is TV. Spending your life in an upholstered chair, eyes glued to an old movie, is *never* going to put any "extras" in your life (except extra pounds!).

Having things to look forward to keeps you alert and enthusiastic. Come on! It's your life. Start planning the extras and give up that crazy notion that the only way you're going to have them is by getting married. As a matter of fact, planning them yourself you *know* they'll happen. Are you so *sure* they would in marriage?

How Can I Tell If a Man Is Interested in Me—or My Financial Situation?

To answer this question, we first have to face a basic truism—women are security oriented. This all-consuming need for security is resting on a framework of carefully constructed fears that we have been fed, that we have imagined, and that we have lived. These fears, unless checked, can make us suspicious, inadequate, timid, cowardly, and eventually neurotic or suicidal.

When a woman goes through a divorce she is granted a certain amount of child support and certain real property, she guards these jealously. If she has no job she is totally dependent on these monies and fearful of their loss.

A widow who receives a substantial life insurance policy, certain real property, perhaps some stocks or interest in a business may well regard herself as a wealthy woman. If she had never held a job she may have an unrealistic attitude about money. She could tenaciously hang on to what she has, becoming quite miserly, or she may spend foolishly, thinking it will go on forever. If you are a formerly married woman who finds herself in an advantageous financial situation, it is certainly a good idea to be wary of the men who are attracted to you. Not all fears or suspicions are unfounded. A comfortably situated woman often does attract unstable men seeking an easy out. Even the divorcée who has very limited means, a small house and a steady job can fall prey to a man looking for a soft berth. It isn't wrong to be on the lookout for such a man. It is wrong to become neurotic about it. To help you make an evaluation of a particular man, here is a check list of the possible danger signals in a relationship.

1. *He always wants to stay at your home*
   The man who never takes you to dinner, to a movie, or to a ball game is a freeloader of the worst sort. Even if he prefers your front room to any place on earth, he should offer to take you out once in awhile. His hesitancy to do so indicates stinginess, thoughtless-

99

ness, lack of imagination, or all three. Could he be avoiding someone, like perhaps creditors or his exwife?

2. *He doesn't discuss his work with you*

In a relationship, it's normal for a man to talk about his work. Even if all he does is complain about his boss, he should have something to say. If he isn't talking it could be he's ashamed of his job. If this is the case there is something wrong with his thinking. Perhaps he may feel you have a better job and he's embarrassed to talk about his. No honest work should ever be a source of embarrassment. Another possibility is the man simply may not have a job. Bring up the subject, as casually as you can, and see what he has to say.

3. *He doesn't have many friends*

It's not just money and possessions that can attract the wrong kind of man. You may have an interesting and varied circle of friends that he covets. When a man has not made friends, it shows a missing link in his character. If a man allows himself to be swallowed up in a woman's world, this indicates he's been a failure in his.

4. *He doesn't introduce you to his family*

A man who's ashamed of his family is a poor husband risk at best. Obviously he feels your relationship might be damaged if you were to meet his relatives. That shows very little faith in you—or himself. He's a man with his values all out of whack.

5. *He comments a great deal on what things cost*

Discussing price indicates a materialistic view of life. This man is either trying to impress you with what he's spent or he's trying to find out what you've spent. In either case things mean a great deal to him—probably more than you do.

6. *He probes into your net worth and that of your family*

Unless you are contemplating marriage with a man, there is no reason he should be inquiring into your net worth. Even if he's a stockbroker or land investor offering you a "good deal," wait until you know him better. If he seems to be a man of means he could be reassuring himself that you are not interested in him for his money.

When he asks you personal financial questions, tell

him you only discuss such things with your lawyer. If he's a sincere man he'll be delighted you're in good hands. If not, the thought of going through a lawyer to get at your money will slow him down.

7. *He wants to be your partner*

When a woman is in business for herself, no matter how small an enterprise, there will always be weak men who are attracted by and to her security. What better job than work for your wife; or sit while she works; or carry her payroll to the bank! Far better that he have a separate job or business during your courtship. It could work into a business relationship later, but first see how he makes it in the business world by himself.

8. *He's borrowed money from you*

A relationship that starts like this will always be in trouble. Is he staying around to get more? Are you putting up with him to get paid back? It's difficult for a relationship to develop normally when such suspicions are in the air. If a man asks to borrow money, tell him your funds are all tied up. That also applies to co-signing anything with him. Tell him your lawyer simply won't let you do that.

9. *He's considerably older—or younger—than you*

Beware! Is he looking for a nurse, a mother—or a wife? If you are a woman of considerable means, have a financial dossier made up on him. When you have money you must learn to think of yourself as a corporation, and follow accepted business methods. Don't shilly-shally because you're afraid you'll "hurt his feelings." Men have great respect for women who handle their business affairs in a businesslike manner.

The two most ordinary fortune hunters in this category are the younger man who plays upon the older woman's vanities and the older man who portrays the role of the darling father. Certainly you have read this plot often enough to recognize it instantly. If not, watch a detective series on television. You'll see variations of it again and again.

10. *He's always trying to sell you something*

Beware of the vendor. As enticing as his wares may be, it's a better idea to consider the man separate from his selling. If you are dating a man who is trying to get you to buy a new insurance policy or a new stock issue, tell him *No* in a way that indicates you sincerely mean *No*. You can tell the insurance man your father or brother handles these matters for you. You can tell the stockbroker you don't enjoy the gamble of the market. Both these *No's* have an air of finality involved.

If you don't do this early in the relationship, you may be plagued by later doubts. When the selling opportunity ceases, his attentions may also cease. If not, you know the man is interested in you, not your checkbook. It is equally unfair to him if you dangle the promise of a sale in front of him. Then the man certainly cannot be blamed for playing the game.

Con artists operate at all levels. A woman alone in her late sixties called me on my radio show to ask if there was anything she could do about a man who had "forced" her to buy an acre of desert land in a new "recreational wonderland." Further questions revealed that the only "force" he had employed was two long lunches and one dinner at which he had promised her her investment would triple in six months! When she tried to put the property on the market she found it was worth less than she paid for it. Now she was facing loss of the land because she couldn't afford to keep up the payments.

For every woman who audibly complains of being "taken advantage of" there are hundreds more who hide their heads in embarrassed silence. Certainly each of us has made smart purchases and a few not so smart. All money is a way of keeping score. Don't waste valuable time feeling remorse over a bad investment. As long as you *learn,* simply count it a valuable lesson.

A classic example of an older woman who pays dearly for attention, is the wealthy divorcée or widow who is constantly decorating her home. The hordes of workmen tramping through to paint, wallpaper, move walls, mirror baths, hang drapes—all offer activity and excitement. The interior decorator, let's say a man considerably younger than she, who entertains her at long client lunches, is forever parading new "finds" in front of her to buy, buy, buy. Of course all this buying is good for the economy, but what a high price to pay for attention! As a financially secure woman you are a target for any number of schemes.

Consider these ten danger signals which will be of

102

help. It's also a good idea to talk things over with a man or woman whose business judgment you value. Romance can cloud your thinking. Certainly you want attention, companionship, and love. But these feelings cannot be *purchased*. No lasting happiness can be achieved with a man you bought and paid for.

There are exceptions to all rules and even all generalities. As I wrote the ten danger signals I could think of three wealthy women who married men they have supported in one way or another for years and these women, to the best of my knowledge, have not been unhappy. One secured a job for her intended in her family's bank, another bought her husband a restaurant to operate, and a third married a tennis instructor and simply travels with him all over the globe.

I had a very frank discussion with the third woman and her philosophy was this: There is a shortage of men at practically every age level. Since she had money she felt she wanted to use it to tip the odds in her favor. She said she couldn't think of anything she'd rather do with her money than travel with a young virile man. It's a strong argument. At least until her money (or his health) gives out.

Money is to be enjoyed, most assuredly, but you need to remove the element of fear. If you are constantly worried that you will lose your money, or that it will be taken from you, you become a prisoner of that money rather than the master of it. To erase fear you have to realize that there is no permanent security in things, and money, property, stocks—all come under the category of things. The only true and lasting security is your *faith* in yourself. Part of that faith should be in your ability to manage your affairs (or find trusted agents to do it for you). The other part of that faith should be your confidence in your ability to manage *without* your money or things should you lose them. Regardless of your monetary situation, you are you. Your happiness and well-being begin and end in your personal attitude about and toward yourself.

I Am So Afraid of a Second Marriage Yet I Don't Like Being Single. How Can I Tell If a Certain Man Is Right for Me?

There is no reason to fear remarriage. There are, however, a great many reasons not to rush into it. A good marriage is the most rewarding living experience ever invented. But being single is far, far superior to a bad marriage. Being single is an enormous challenge and the perfect time to spend on you, your present career, and your future plans.

Whether a certain man is right for you is a separate problem. Certainly you should fear remarriage with the wrong man. No test, as to who is right and who is wrong, is totally reliable. (In *The Divorcée's Handbook* I stated that never-married men over thirty-six were poor marriage risks, then I married a forty-one-year-old bachelor! Ours is truly a great marriage.)

There are, however, certain determinations you can make before marriage that can save you possible heartache. Establish in your head (not heart) what you are looking for in a man. This doesn't mean height, weight, and color of eyes. In doing research for this book I sent out a questionnaire to formerly married women throughout the country. One question stated: *To rate what you are looking for in a man, number the following in order of importance to you:*

_____Financial Security

_____Sexual Compatibility

_____Mutual interest (sports, hobbies, etc.)

_____Religious compatibility

_____Good stepfather for your children

_____Good looks

_____Well educated

_____Exciting life

_____Well-mannered

_____Companionship
_____Personal neatness
_____Other:_____

Use this test to rate what you are looking for in a man, what is important to you, what is not so important, what excites you, what absolutely turns you off. After you complete the list, examine your answers with these ideas in mind, starting with the first category.

1. If financial security is important to you, do not consider marriage with a man who has difficulty holding a job. You will nag him unmercifully.
2. If sexual compatibility has high priority, don't consider a man unable to bring you to your full enjoyment potential. This marriage would be in trouble.
3. If you have a sport or a hobby which means a great deal to you and nothing to the man in your life, this by itself is not too serious. But his *attitude* is. If you enjoy tennis but he gets jealous when you play with men, you had better resolve that situation before marriage.
4. If you are devoutly religious and he is lukewarm, this is no problem unless he discourages your church attendance. If you are a member of a faith that only recognizes marriage with a partner of the same faith, this would definitely be something to watch out for.
5. If you have children it is of course desirable to marry someone who cares about them. But don't consider a man just because he is kind to your children.
6. If a man's physical looks are important you probably are terribly insecure. Of course it's divine to be seen with a handsome man, but looks by themselves cannot sustain *any* relationship.
7. Educational background is one area to consider seriously. If you are university-educated and enjoy intellectual pursuits you are not going to be able to sustain a relationship with an uneducated man unless he has made up for his lack of formal education by self-education. Although seldom given as a cause for divorce, intellectual incompatibility shows up again and again and again as a strong contributing and underlying problem in a troubled marriage.
8. Some women are so bored with their lives that they dream of marriage with a man who has a fascinating

position, travels, entertains lavishly, and who can create for them the atmosphere they are unable to create for themselves. What these women forget is that in order to attract such a man they must have something to offer. If an exciting life is important to you, concentrate on developing yourself into a fascinating person.

9. Good manners are the niceties of civilization. Good manners smooth social intercourse. Good manners lessen tensions and calm ruffled feathers. I love a well-mannered man. To me good manners are indicative of a good outlook—in either men or women.

10. Companionship certainly should be an integral part of any good relationship. Without it there is no relationship. But to consider marriage based solely on the need for a companion, is settling for less than marriage has to offer.

11. If your first husband was a terrible slob, perhaps you are looking for a man who hangs up his wet towel, puts his dirty socks in the hamper and washes his own dishes after a snack. When tidiness is inherent in your nature, it's difficult to live with a messy person.

The results I received from the questionnaires were very, very interesting. "Financial security" was always in the top four. "Sexual compatability" and "Companionship" were usually in the top four. "Religion" was either at the top of the list or near the bottom, which indicates the part it plays in peoples' lives. "Good looks" hardly mattered at all.

The next question I put to the women was: *If it meant marriage, would you lessen your requirement in these areas:* Answer *yes or no.*

_____Sex
_____Financial
_____Religious

By this question I meant to find out how much remarriage meant to each woman. These are also questions you should ask yourself. Would you marry a man with whom your sexual response was less than terrific? Would you marry a man if you knew your life together would be a struggle? Would you marry a man of another faith or no religion at all?

Of all the answers I received, no woman was willing to lessen her requirements in "Sexual compatibility." A few said they would lessen their "Financial" requirement, but the majority said "Religious."

The next question I asked each woman was what she felt was the *single most necessary attribute* a man could possess. "Compassion" was the winner, closely followed by "consideration," "sensitivity," and "maturity." This is also a good test to give yourself. What do you find about certain men that is very attractive? It could be a quick mind, gentleness, sense of humor. Think about it.

The antithesis of this was, of course, the next question: *What do you find* missing *in most men you date?* And the winner was—maturity. Runners up were honesty, stability, high morals, and unselfishness. Do you find yourself agreeing with most of the answers?

I also asked the women what things men did that turned them off. A goodly number said they were tired of men who only asked them out to take them to bed. Some complained of dull conversation, lack of initiative, loudness, and self-centeredness.

The questionnaire was seven pages long. By the time I had carefully read through the pages I was more than casually acquainted with each woman. I knew her background, her work history, her first husband, her children, her problems, her fears, her hopes and her desires. By honestly answering these questions about yourself, you should be able to tell what kind of man you are seeking.

Where *are* these men? Nearly every woman filling out the questionnaire complained that they were scarce, scarce, scarce. Nearly every questionnaire ended with a plea of some sort.

"I want a man with strength of character."
"Where are all the courageous souls!"
"Is there such a thing as a man at peace with himself?"

From the general sameness of so many comments there does seem to be a shortage of secure men in our culture.

Is there something wrong with the way we, as mothers, rear our sons? So many of the missing virtues listed were virtues that should have been learned at home. Perhaps as unhappily married women we subconsciously take it out on our male offspring. Many, many women suffer from acute inferiority complexes. This must do something to male children. Perhaps one of the greatest services we could perform for future womanhood is to take particular care to instill manhood in our sons.

I can't help but agree with most of the answers given on the questionnaire. A good man *is* hard to find. A kind, mature male with compassion and integrity is not standing on every street corner. A sensitive lover with concern for the woman and her needs is indeed rare. An intellectually stimulating companion who can admire your mind without pawing your body is not at every office party. If I sound pro woman it's only because I am. Very much so.

In fairness to men I asked my participants: *If you were to marry again, what would you do differently?* Here is the way the answers went: "Try harder"; "Communicate honestly"; and "Not take him for granted." As one highly literate music teacher wrote, "Not treat love as a permanent, imperishable thing." It does take two, working full time, to keep a relationship alive and well. Until such time as you find a compatible male, what are you going to do? Sit and fret because you haven't found him? Curse your single life? Wallow in self-pity? Tread water in your career until someone rescues you? I hope not, for your sake as well as the future "he."

Life is a series of changes. And change is a chance to grow. As you concentrate on building for yourself the best life obtainable, your demands in a man will change. When you become financially sound by working at a stimulating exciting job will you be so quick to jump into a marriage just for security? As your mind develops and your interests widen, are you going to be satisfied with a man who wants to spend his evenings glued to the TV?

You know for certain that the one person you *will* be spending the rest of your life with, is you. So isn't it in your best interest to make yourself an enjoyable person? People at peace with themselves are attractive people—attractive to themselves and to others. Don't make the judgment now that you are afraid of a second marriage. This indicates a possibility of failure. Rather say to yourself: This is my life and I love it. If I meet a man and marry, I want to marry the man, not the state of matrimony.

I Am a Widow Who Intends Never to Marry Again. What Future Plans Should I Be Making?

Surely the decision not to marry again is yours to make. It is a personal decision affecting no one but you. Therefore I would not discuss your feelings with your friends. You want to continue to be invited to do things with them and unfortunately most people think in twos. Why limit your social engagements by announcing your future plans. You don't commit to marriage by accepting a dinner date.

By choosing to remain single it is very important that your future be not only planned, but *well* planned. If you are a working widow you should know exactly how many more years you can work at your present job. You should know exactly when your retirement begins and what funds you will receive. You should know where you are going to live and exactly what it is going to cost you to live. With the steady inflation in this country I would strongly advise you to plan a retirement well within your expected means.

Another hedge against inflation is to plan now for parttime work that you can do when you retire. If you have office skills perhaps you can do typing in your home or work for a church or oganization that has a limited amount of correspondence and bookkeeping. If you sew, a good dressmaker is always in demand. If you cook, consider catering in private homes. With so many mothers working, a good reliable sitter can practically fill her calendar a month in advance. Keeping in the mainstream of life is as important as the money it brings in.

If you are a widow who doesn't work, it is doubly important that your life be planned. Know what monies and property you have and what your potential is. Don't risk any of your capital in ventures you know nothing about. Even if your son-in-law wants to open a fried chicken franchise, refer him to the bank. Now is *not* the time in your life to gamble.

If you have inherited common stock I would recommend that you take a course in how the stock market operates. Call the largest brokerage firm in your area and ask them about it. I would continue to work with the broker your husband used, but I would *certainly* take the course also. It is *always* smart to know where your money is and how it is doing.

If you are a widow who owns her own home you might consider selling it and buying a condominium or a small home in a leisure development. I have known widows who have been extremely happy in these areas and widows who have hated it. Here are some of the pros and cons.

Pros:
1. No heavy maintenance. The grounds are cared for, repairs made and buildings painted.
2. Maximum security. The grounds are usually fenced or walled with a main gate. When you leave for a trip you simply lock your front door.
3. No small children. The noise factor is practically non-existent, no bicycles to drive over, no roughhousing in the swimming pool.
4. Planned activity. Most developments have golf courses, pools, recreational centers, even restaurants, and excursions.
5. Resident medical care. The larger developments have medical and dental offices as well as the usual shopping centers.
6. Constant source of companionship.

Cons:
1. The architectural sameness often gives one the feeling of an institution. Because of the general upkeep individual gardens are often limited to pots of geraniums on a balcony.
2. Because of the "village" feeling your comings and goings are known by all. Also, most developments are quite far from the center of town and central transportation.
3. Limiting the age limit can have the effect of making the community look like a geriatric center.
4. Too much organization can rob you of individual choice. When all around you is leisure activity it's hard to concentrate on a job or work at home.

5. Having all your basic needs met can keep you a voluntary prisoner. Some women have told me they feel debilitated by the air of "constant care."
6. Although there is constant companionship it's not particularly of your own choosing. Retirement communities are group marriages. One widower told me he didn't think of himself as old until he moved into a leisure village and looked around. He decided to move back to an apartment at the beach where there were people of all ages.

Before you make the decision to buy into one of these developments, talk to people who now live there. See if you can rent a home or apartment of someone who is going on a trip. The more research you can do, the better decision you will make.

As a woman who intends not to marry again, it's vital that you have interesting hobbies that you can pursue on your own. Once you have retired, time will slip by if you don't plan your days. Most "time experts" say we let our life slip by in wasted minutes. Actually sitting down and making advance plans is a must. List the things you want to accomplish this year. Then make a two-year plan, a five-year plan, a ten-year plan. At first you'll just look at the blank piece of paper and wonder what in the world you will be doing in five years!

Keep your lists in a notebook and go over them the first Monday of every month. Draw a red line through the goals you have accomplished, add new ones, rearrange time schedules. The more you work on the list the more interesting things you'll think of to do. Read your newspaper very carefully to see what events are coming to town, what courses are starting, what groups need help, who is running for office and what books are new and recommended. See what travel suggestions appeal to you. Think of which friends you would like to invite for dinner or to spend the weekend.

Planning *really* is a vital part of creative living. There is time to do all you want to do. Having goals makes it a pleasure to get up in the morning. Learning new things keeps you mentally alive. Looking forward keeps you young. You are not here to be at the convenience of anyone but yourself. Each age has glorious rewards. Start making the good things happen to you—now, *and* in the future.

I Am Over Forty and the Single Men My Age Are Only Interested in Younger Women.
How Can I Compete with These Women?

There are over 40 million women over forty in this country today—single, married, divorced, or widowed. And the projection is for another 3 million by 1975. There are 36 million men over forty—single, married, divorced, or widowed. So the competition is very keen, not just bcause of the younger women but because of the shortage of men!

In the nineteenth century, forty was woman's life expectancy. Today, forty is the half-way mark. This is why it is so absolutely vital that the single woman of *whatever* age have her feet on the ground, her life organized, and her interests *not* dependent upon men. You cannot count on remarriage. And you shouldn't. Waiting in a state of limbo, directing all your activities toward finding a man, robs you of the chance of real happiness, and actually *lessens* your chances of remarriage.

To explain this statement, let's look at the reasons men give for dating younger women:

1. *The younger woman is more interesting and enthusiastic*

   The younger woman often *is* more interesting and enthusiastic. Age and problems do weigh a woman down. A young woman can sustain a social life that an older woman would find tiring or boring. It's not always physical age but rather mental attitude that creates enthusiasm. An older woman has "been there before" and finds it a task to gush over an invitation to a football game.

2. *The younger woman is less complicated*

   Giving this as a reason would indicate that the man

has problems of his own. He wants a good time with no involvement. There is nothing wrong with this. He may have just come out of a divorce and doesn't want to listen to anyone else's problems. He wants to go sailing or skiing or on long walks in the country. But not with a woman worrying about the sitter she has for her kids, what she's going to fix for dinner, and how she's going to hem her skirt before work Monday morning. He wants to escape with a companion who's a free soul.

3. *The younger woman doesn't push so hard for marriage*

It's easier to understand this reason when you examine the moral code of the younger woman. A woman over forty was reared in an entirely different attitude. Marriage for her is the Alpha and Omega. Today's younger woman considers marriage as *one* of the options open to her.

4. *The younger woman is more independent*

Younger women *are* more independent. Today's young woman is career oriented and much more self-sufficient. She moves around with an enviable ease and has decidedly *lessened* her dependence upon men. Her work is meaningful and she is becoming increasingly aware of her ability to make her way in the world, on her own.

5. *The younger woman is in better physical shape*

This reason brings us down to the nitty-gritty. The younger woman *is* usually in better shape. She cares how she looks and works at it. Plus the fact of life that a younger woman *is* a younger woman. No amount of face peeling or leg kicking is going to make *you* twenty-six and her forty-three.

6. *The younger woman flatters the ego*

The company of the younger woman does flatter the male ego. This is probably the most honest reason. Add to this the fact that the practice of men marrying younger women has been historically sanctioned. Society has always accepted as natural the age span between men and women, provided the man is older. But let a woman marry a younger man and the tongues wag.

113

Now, as a woman over forty, how do you counteract the younger woman? What magic formula do you apply to your life to put you in the running? To help you become a more desirable woman let's go back over these reasons and see where you fit in.

1. *The younger woman is more interesting and enthusiastic.*

We'll start with reason number one. Being an enthusiastic and interesting woman should not depend on age. If it did, age should work to your advantage. The process of physically aging should in no way affect your growth mentally. If your learning processes stopped in your first marriage, now is the time to charge up your brain again.

Keep informed of what's going on in the world. Make an effort to learn something about the various businesses with which you come in contact. If you are a secretary for a Savings and Loan Company, find out what a building contractor does. When one comes in for a loan, you will then have something to say and be able to ask an intelligent question.

Enthusiasm is your mental attitude toward life. If you dwell upon your problems they will show on your face, come out in your speech, and decidedly dull your verve. This doesn't mean you must be perpetually smiling or punctuate every sentence with a nervous laugh. What it does mean is when you are with a man try to be *pleased* as well as pleasing.

If you date a man who is a quiet person and who never seems to suggest *anything* you can be enthusiastic about, help him. Suggest something that appeals to you. He may be new at being single and just waiting to be pulled into the mainstream. Your enthusiasms could awaken his. Enthusiasm is catching.

2. *The younger woman is less complicated*

Certainly the younger woman is less complicated, if "complicated" means involved. The formerly married woman over forty is totally involved in her life and well you should be. Your life must have purpose and direction. You can't be available at the sound of the telephone to drop everything and run and play. If complicated means "problem-laden" then you probably fit this description also. But it should not be general knowledge, dinner table conversation, or the first thing you say when you answer the door. A man spends his day coping with the business world and he doesn't want to be hit with problems at night.

The majority of single men over forty are divorced or widowed. You don't know what conflict a man has lived through. He may be totally unequipped to handle any involvement or responsibility. This is not your problem. It's his. You know where you're going and you don't have time to stop what you're doing to straighten him out. That doesn't mean you can't date him occasionally. It does mean that you shouldn't enforce a relationship he is unable to handle. Each person has the responsibility to work out his own destiny.

Some men want absolutely no emotional involvement with women because they are immature boys. When they say they like the younger woman because she is "uncomplicated," they mean they like her because she is "available" and "undemanding." This man is certainly not for you. He wants a "good time" with no promises, no involvement. He wants someone when *he* wants them and then disappears when it's over.

The single woman over forty cannot be a playmate. In the first place the competition in that field will kill you. Youth is a must and even if you lasted a couple of years there is a constant parade of new beauties. Eventually you would wake-up out of the running and come to grips with the unpleasant facts of where you are and what you have become.

3. *The younger woman doesn't push for marriage*

I think this reason should be reworded: the younger woman doesn't push *as hard* for marriage. Age can panic you. Age can quicken the pace. The younger woman knows she has more years to play the field. The older woman gets down to the basics. The younger woman enjoys the chase game. The older woman knows it's nonsense. The younger woman thinks marriage might be fun *someday*. The older woman knows it's the mature way to live.

As a woman over forty, your primary energy drive should be: You pushing *you*. Not a shove into marriage but a genuine drive to create for yourself the best possible world. Your job should never be neglected for social activity. Your home standards should not be lowered in an effort to "have more fun." Your goals should not be tampered with for "expediency."

Most women don't marry well because they "settle" for less than they want. Setting standards for yourself lets the world know what you think of yourself. Therefore you don't have to push for marriage—you will be sought after. Maybe you won't have the quantity of men surrounding you that surround the younger woman, but you'll have the quality.

4. *The younger woman is more independent*

Probably. You are more independent than your mother and certainly your girls will be more emancipated than you. If man's greatest battle has been "know thyself," woman's surely must be "find thyself."

When a man refers to a woman as "independent" he usually means she doesn't fit into the ordinary "accepted" patterns. He indicates that she governs her own life and doesn't "depend" upon men. This is certainly admirable and to be encouraged. It works well and is intriguing to men.

As a formerly married woman (of whatever age) you have come to the end of one "ordinary" accepted pattern. Your role as wife is over. Now what? You can assume any number of new roles. However, I would certainly urge you to first "find thyself." Developing an independent attitude is a good start. Continuing to *act* like a wife with the men you meet is wrong. Trying to fit each new date into old behavior patterns, is wrong. "Leaning" on men before you are invited to lean, is wrong.

Remember, most single men over forty have been married. A great many are afraid they'll fall into the same "trap." Your sense of independence reassures them that you aren't perishing to marry again. Independence is right for you anyway. Step right out there, it's your life!

5. *A younger woman is in better physical shape*

Okay. But how do you look? Are you overdoing or underdoing? These are the two categories where most women over forty make their biggest mistakes.

Overdoing: This means trying too hard to look younger. Bleached or dyed hair. Too much or not enough makeup. Kooky clothes. Juvenile attitude. Be honest. You know

116

what I mean. Overdoing has the *exact* opposite effect it intends. Instead of looking younger you look foolish.

Underdoing: Letting yourself "go" is underdoing. Excess weight, old-fashioned hairdo, dowdy clothes, sluggish walk, downturned mouth. It's never too late to turn a new leaf. Don't wait for New Years Eve to make those resolutions about yourself. Could you stand to lose a few pounds? Then do it! A few minutes a day in regular exercise is a good place to start.

A session with a good hair stylist is well worth the money. But make it *very clear* from the start that you are a working woman on a budget and you want something you can handle yourself. Then go to the cosmetic department of a large store next time they have free makeup demonstrations. Even if you don't like everything they do to you, you'll pick up a few pointers.

I see no reason not to avail yourself of the new advances in plastic surgery. If you would like puffy eyelids smoothed, a "crepe-y" neck tightened or a complete face-life—do it. I would suggest that you do it quietly and not discuss it with family or friends. Remember, what you think and feel will register on your face. Don't hang on to bad thoughts. They will undo even the most expensive surgeon's work.

You can compete quite well with the younger women when you act your age, not hers. What you have to offer only you can offer. Each day offers new opportunities for you to add to your life. Every woman grows older. Few grow more interesting.

6. *A younger woman flatters the ego*

Every man dating a much younger woman will admit this. After they have given all the other reasons they kid themselves with, they will eventually add, "She

117

makes me feel younger, she makes me feel proud." Here's a man who hasn't grown up, just grown older.

I asked a forty-seven-year-old man I considered quite successful and attractive why he dates girls in the nineteen to twenty-two category. I told him he certainly must wonder if they would continue to date him if he weren't a wealthy and successful man. "Isn't this debilitating to you as a man?," I finally concluded. "Yes," he answered after a long pause, "but not at the time."

"At the time" a man is dating much younger women, forget him for a while. It's obviously something he must "go through." Some men continue this pattern, widening the gap with every year. They are not for you. Why waste your time in a league where you couldn't possibly win. Most real men, however, do tire of this playground and pick for their permanent companion a woman nearer their own age.

If you are a woman in your forties why not date men in their fifties or even sixties? Forget the numerical age and concentrate on inner qualities. A man can be dull and boring at thirty and fascinating at sixty. If you are equating a man's age with his sexual powers, forget it. A man can be as great a lover at sixty-five as he was at twenty-five—and often better!

Pay attention to yourself and what you have to offer. *You are in great demand.* That is, if you are an interesting, enthusiastic, independent woman courageously leading your life with style—and if you've made an effort to keep in good physical shape. Men, real men, will be attracted to you, not for what you can do for them but because *you are who you are.*

So don't dwell on your age. Develop your interests. Concentrate on your career. Build your self-image. Youth, by itself, can't sustain much of anything. But *style* stands all the tests—especially the test of time.

How Should I Handle the Advances of Married Men?

Parrying the advances of married men is one of the unwelcome tasks of the formerly married woman. It's not just the husbands of your friends who will give you trouble. Some married men you meet at work will consider you fair game. Married men you meet at a party or taking a class or walking your dog may be attracted to you. Regardless of how circumspect your behavior, there are *some* married men who consider all divorcées and widows worth a try.

Of course it's a good feeling to be attractive to men, married or otherwise. But to consider an involvement with a married man is a waste of time and energy. It's far better to cut them off immediately rather than play along for the fun of it. How you turn them down is important. I've divided the married men into classic groups, with suggestions of how best to handle their advances.

1. *The nice man at work*

   It takes awhile for this married man to state his case. First he endears himself to you with thoughtful little deeds. He's always storybook polite, anxious to help, and enormously kind. How can you not be attracted to a man like this! When he does ask you for a drink after work, you really can't refuse. After all, he's such a nice man.

   If, after the drink, he suggests other meetings, decline. Tell him he's a dear person but you haven't time to hold his hand. If you don't you will find him taking every minute he can steal. He isn't being fair to you. While he is playing at playing, you are being kept out of circulation. He goes home to a wife. You go home alone.

2. *The unhappily married man*

   Every divorcée, eventually, meets a genuinely unhappy married man who is suffering in a bad marriage. Although this man will talk about it and complain bitterly, remind yourself that he is *still* married. This kind of situation can be tempting to the divorcée who would like to date this man were he single. Because of his apparent disgust with his marriage she feels no guilt in sympathizing with him. She listens to his problems, tells him he's a wonderful person and keeps hoping he'll leave home and come to her.

This situation is a trap. Chances are he is *not* going to leave his wife or he would have done so. He is enjoying his martyrdom enormously or he wouldn't have created it. He is using you to toy with freedom. You are his outlet, his ego-builder, his escape.

Even if this man were to get a divorce while you are involved with him, there is no guarantee he would jump into a total relationship with you. Once he has grabbed at freedom he is going to want to enjoy it for a while. Meanwhile you have been wasting your time in an involvement that can only work to your disadvantage. Whether he stays married or gets divorced, you are in for heartache. If you happen to know his wife you have forfeited a friend in the bargain.

3. *"Look, we can do it and not get involved"*

This man has at least put his cards on the table and approached you with a basically honest proposal. He is suggesting that the two of you assume an "adult posture" and fill each others "needs." He needs an away-from-home sex life and you need male companionship and comfort. Sound reasonable? Yes, except for one small point. He can do it and not get involved. Can you?

Most relationships between a married man and a single woman do start this way. They like each others' company. He has made no promises. She has made no demands. All *that*, however, is in the beginning. Few women can handle such a relationship for very long. Even the most coldly rational couple I've ever met who attempted this arrangement finally had to call it quits. He was a computer scientist and she an archeologist. They had no money problems, travel together was easily arranged, and they lived in different states. He had no major problem at home. He simply found her fascinating. She was bored with the men she was dating and found him exciting. As mature adults they knew they could handle everything.

And they did. For a while. Then came the holidays

and she was lonely. She took a hotel room in his town. He became nervous and irritable. What had been a delightful escape became an unwanted burden. As she later said to me, "He was unable to make a total commitment to me or his wife. I realized that I wanted a man who wanted me with equal force."

Don't make the mistake of thinking you can have an affair with a married man and not have emotional problems. You can't. When a man suggests this, tell him you want a whole man in a total commitment. He can't help but admire such a stand.

4. A friend's husband

You need all your married women friends. You need them as friends and as allies. It is through your married friends that a good part of your social life is kept alive. How you handle the advances of their husbands is quite different from how you treat the man whose wife is unknown to you.

Your friends' husbands are likely to be teases who only make a try for you at a social gathering. They will hold you close on a dance floor, corner you for a kiss in the kitchen, put a hand on your knee under the dinner table. They really don't mean business. At the first opportunity tell them so. You have no place in your life for cut-ups.

It's important, however, that you don't put a man down in front of his wife. All he has to do, when he gets home, is tell his wife you started it. This could cause a breach in your friendship and damage your reputation with other wives. No woman wants a single woman around who is an obvious male-chaser. Therefore, the best way to conduct your life around your married friends is to live by the following suggestions:

a. Don't initiate time alone with your friends' husbands

There are some divorced women who have a way of asking for attention from married men. When the situation gets out of hand these same women will roll their eyes in amazement, claiming they didn't mean "to start anything." The widow who asks her friend's husband to stop by on his way home from work to look at her furnace, is allowing a "situation" to happen. Even if the request were genuine, she is to blame if he puts the move on her.

He could have been thinking about her for weeks and wondering how to get her alone. When she calls, he assumes that her thoughts have been about him also.

Casual encounters are almost as dangerous. If you are shopping and run into a friend's husband, don't accept his offer to buy you a cup of coffee or a drink. He may be the grandest guy in the world, but it just isn't worth it. You can't possibly predict how his wife will react if she were to find out, or how the story would be told by mutual "friends" who might chance by.

I'm not saying this social structure is right or wrong. It's simply how it is. You can defy "the group" stating they are restrictive, old-fashioned and narrow-minded. Just keep in mind, however, that you need them more than they need you. If you are going to be a part of a married social life you have to play by *their* rules.

b. *Don't call a friend's husband at his office*

There is no reason to call a friend's husband at his office unless you are a paying customer. Even in a business situation you can't predict smooth sailing. Men can be every bit as gossipy and petty as women when they decide to be so. You never know when a husband will taunt his wife with a "guess who called me at the office today?" It may be a harmless "keep-her-on-her-toes" jest, but it starts her mind rolling in a new direction. She immediately begins to wonder why he said it, what the phone conversation was about, and if you can be counted upon to be *all* business.

I strongly recommend that you do business with men you don't see socially as someone's husband. The classified section of the phone book contains all the help you could possibly need. Of course, there are women, secure in their marriage, who would be hurt if you broke off business relations with their husbands because you were afraid of gossip. You must judge each situation individually and make transitions gradually.

c. *Don't single out a friend's husband for a personal discussion*

Seeing couples socially and men singularly in a business situation, you have occasion to discuss many things. After all, that's what social inter-course is all about. Talking to people is marvelous. Talking to people is invigorating, informative, and entertaining. Keep it that way with your friend's husband. Avoid discussions that dwell on your life, your problems, your children's problems. Avoid talking about your former husband, or the current man in your life. Personal discussions suggest an air of intimacy.

Equally as dangerous is to encourage a friend's husband to talk about *his* personal problems. You may be the one person he can "really talk to." Can you imagine the repercussions if he announces this bit of information to his wife? It's also bad form to listen to a husband downgrade his wife. You don't know all the facets of their married life and any comments you could make would be invalid. If the wife in question happens to be a close friend of yours, she would be extremely hurt if you agreed with her husband's criticism of her, just or unjust.

Far better to keep discussions with husbands lim-ited to politics and religion and forget sex and per-sonal relationships.

d. *Don't create the image that single life is a ball*
Always bubbling into your married friends' homes and parties as if you didn't have a care in the world, gives you the air of a scatterbrain and a flirt. I don't mean for you to walk around looking like you had the cares of the world on your shoul-ders. Nobody wants a moody unhappy woman around. But neither do they want some gay sprite with a false bouyancy rattling nonsense at their din-ner table.

Acting giddy makes your friends wonder just what *is* going on. What are you doing and who are you seeing that makes you act so strangely around them? Are you perhaps having an affair with some-one in the group? You could be totally innocent, di-vinely happy, and genuinely pleased with your life and be thought a shallow person wallowing in trivi-ality just because you're out of character. Some husband, for extramarital activity, could figure you're just the playmate he's been looking for.

You are you, divorced or widowed. You don't need to develop a new personality to match your new living arrangement. Everyone knows being single is hard. But again, that doesn't mean it's debilitating. Concentrate on the positive aspects. One of the positive aspects is enjoying new male friends as friends. Because they are men is no reason to approach them as the predatory female. Just because you're in a dating situation is no cause to treat all men as prospective dates.

e. *Nip him in the bud*

Since he has been so stupid and selfish as to make a move on a friend of his wife's, be very specific with him. Tell him you don't know where he got the idea you cared about him other than as a friend. Make it clear you are still his friend but you don't want any hanky-panky now—or ever. Tell him to forget the whole thing and you will too. If he doesn't believe you and continues to bother you, get a bit more tough. When he calls you at home tell him to stop or you'll call him at *his* home. *That* message should be clear enough to slow down any would-be Romeo.

f. *Don't overreact*

If you are approached by a friend's husband at a social gathering, don't make a scene. A slap, tears, and cries of indignation are *not* in order. When you become dramatic you call attention to an unfortunate incident. You force everyone within hearing to react also. Deserved or undeserved, permanent harm could come of such an outcry. You want to get out of the situation as best you can, not go out of your way to make it worse.

Another overreaction is to laugh at your suitor and puncture him with such statements as, "You and me—are you kidding?" "You creep, what makes you think I'd be interested in you!" "You mean she lets you *out* at night?"

No man likes to be put down by being belittled. Not only have you turned him off but quite probably you have turned him into an enemy. Men gossips are just as vicious as women gossips. Whenever your name comes up you can bet he won't have many nice things to say about you. If his wife should ever know how you made fun of him she will be even more cruel. No one likes to be married to a man her friends think is a creep!

g. *Don't discuss it*

After you have refused an overture from a friend's husband, forget it. Do not discuss it with anyone. If you tell a mutual friend you run the risk of it being spread around. After all, it's a choice bit of gossip. Don't kid yourself that you need to ask a friend for advice. You know you did the right thing to refuse and you will know how to handle it in the future. "Asking advice" is an old ruse for "telling."

The person you must not discuss it with at all costs is the man's wife. There is nothing on your conscience that needs clearing. Why go out of your way to cause trouble. If you tell a wife her husband made a pass at you, you force her to react to the situation. A typical reaction, after she has discussed it with her husband, is to lash out at you. She could change the story to cover her hurt by making you the aggressor. This could put your social life back quite a few notches. Who wants a single woman around who's on the prowl for husbands?

5. *A man who's on the fence*

If you meet a man who shows great interest in you, yet whom you feel is married, it's best to find out immediately. The easiest and most direct way is to ask him. If he says *No*, that's great. If he says *Yes*, he's married, you will know what to do. But if he starts to give you all sorts of "descriptions of conditions" you'll have to tell him to be more specific. Here are the usual lines:

a. *"I'm separated."*

A man who tells you he's separated, isn't telling you anything. "Separated" could mean his wife has gone to the hairdressers or it could mean he's moved into an apartment. Ask him which kind of separation he means. The only kind of separation meaningful to you would be if divorce papers have been filed.

Even a "trial separation" is not good enough. Suppose you become really serious about him and he decides to go home "and try again." You could be in a yo-yo arrangement with this man for literally years and never resolve anything. The most "advanced" case of this I know of is a man rearing two families. One family of three children is legally his and the other child he has by another woman. He "separates" from his wife for months at a time

125

but he has never made the final move. After the birth of the child, the single woman was trapped into this unfair circumstance and continues to go along with it. Do you think he'll ever divorce his wife and marry her?

b. *"I'm in litigation."*

If you have been through a legal divorce, and you know the ropes, pin him down. Litigation could mean he's being sued for drunk driving. Ask him what type of litigation he's involved in, where it stands, and where it's going. His answer could be that his wife is refusing a divorce, they can't agree on a property settlement, or his lawyer told him not to leave home until the papers are signed.

Check out his answer. Your lawyer can see if he's in litigation. Don't feel underhanded about it. There is no reason for him to treat you like a dummy and withhold information. After all, you have a right to know what you're getting into with him. If he sincerely cares about you he will appreciate your interest. If he doesn't, he'll back off.

c. *"I have an arrangement."*

Some married couples actually do have an "arrangement" that allows them equal freedom to pursue "outside interests." Whether it's the thrill of knowing what the other partner is doing, the shared secrets, or the thumbing of their collective noses at tradition, it's obviously the macabre that keeps them together. You want no part of this.

Some couples have less-complicated arrangements. Staying together until the children are grown is one. If you meet a man who offers this as his excuse for staying married, point out to him that children are far more damaged in an unhappy household than they are by divorce. He won't agree with you because he has convinced himself that he is a martyr. He also doesn't want a divorce. Playing is much more fun.

6. *A man you think is hiding something*

This brings us to the man who tells you he isn't married, but in your bones you feel he is. It's quite easy to check him out. Call his home during the day. Drive by his address. Ask someone who knows him.

If he has a suppressed phone number, you don't know his address, and you haven't met any of his friends, he must be hiding something. You can look at his car registration, check with people where he works or hire a private detective, if you want to go that far. Frankly, such a secretive person is a bad risk. Suggest some basic honesty between the two of you. If he can't give you his phone number, he can't offer you much of anything else.

Before we leave the married man and go on to the next question, let's talk about a husband of a friend of yours who *does* get a divorce and then who *does* ask you out. Should you date him? The first thing to consider is who means the most to you—your friend or her husband. It's extremely difficult to have both.

If you choose to date the man, be ready for gossip. Mutual friends will wonder if you had anything to do with the divorce. Mutual married women friends will hesitate to ask you to parties. Mutual friends will take sides. Of course it's quite possible for the two of you to make all new friends. Just be sure you accept that first date with your eyes open. What you are prepared for hurts less.

No matter what I say, or anyone else for that matter, if you want to have an affair with a married man, you will. All any one can do for you is give both sides of the picture. The disadvantages far outweigh the advantages. The pain is greater than the pleasure. Haven't you had enough pain in your life already?

I Have Been in Love with a Married Man for Several Months. He Has Promised to Divorce His Wife and Marry Me, but He Keeps Putting It Off.
What Should I Do?

The best way to decide what to do about this man is to be totally objective about the relationship. Unless you are, you can't possibly make the right decision. When you say you "love" him, what are you actually saying? Love can be a synonym we use to replace such words as: need, depend upon, desire, want, or have-grown-accustomed-to. To help you be objective, answer these few questions regarding the relationship.

1. Does he support you?
2. Does he spend his vacation with you?
3. Does he spend holidays with you?
4. Does he allow you to date others?
5. Does he encourage you in your work?

These are the types of questions you *must* ask yourself. Otherwise you will let that one tiny word "love" keep you a prisoner of his indecision. Certainly you have a wonderful time together and you're lonesome when he leaves. But then what? Do you have interesting work to do or is your life built totally around him? Are you "counting" on his marrying you to give you a purpose in life?

The only way you can benefit from this relationship is if you treat it the way *he* does. His work is important to him and so yours should be equally important to you. He has another life with his wife and so you should have another life with other men. He can't seem to decide what he wants so

128

why should you totally commit yourself. He wants his freedom to come and go and so you should have yours. Since he spends a good deal of time in your company he should contribute to your living expenses. If you are always cooking for him, he should buy the food, the liquor, and the wine. "Several" months is a big investment in a man.

The divorce rate continues to go up steadily. This man may leave his wife, or be asked to leave. *Or* he may not. If he does, are you ready to go through his divorce with him? When things go wrong he will blame you. He will transfer his guilt feelings to your shoulders. He will accuse you of alienating him from his children. Then once he's free, he may decide that's the way he wants it. Marriage with you may become the furthest thing from his mind.

As a woman alone, a good relationship with a man is a very desirable thing. But when the relationship is built on dishonesty it's time to ask questions. You haven't the time to invest in a man who can't make up his mind. Your life must be more precious to you. You should be concentrating these efforts on developing your potential. If this man truly cares about you he should encourage you to express yourself. I'm sure you know in your heart what is the best thing for you to do about this man and this relationship. "Several months" is a long time with one man which makes "cutting it off" not such an easy job.

There is, however, a definite plan of action you could follow that will resolve the problem. By following these suggestions you will be leading a very constructive life. By following these suggestions he will resolve his problems and marry you or he will find another playmate. In any event *you* will be free of this heartache.

1. *Stop mentioning marriage*

No amount of haranguing, pleading, threatening, or cajoling is going to force a man to leave his wife. He will leave when he wants to leave. All you are doing is making him and yourself miserable. The desire to be nagged was certainly not what attracted this man to you. He gets nagging at home.

Not mentioning marriage and divorce will be a relief to this man. He is aware of how everybody feels. You are aware of how everybody feels. Only talk about pleasant subjects that interest you. Ask him for business advice, suggestions of what kind of work you should do, courses you should take at night school. Everyone loves to be asked their opinion.

2. *Re-evaluate your direction*

Look hard at your job. You need it. If you don't have a job, get one tomorrow. No, this afternoon! Take a volunteer job at the hospital if you don't need money. Look at the next job up the ladder and start planning what you must do to get there. Start thinking in terms of what you want to be doing a year from now. Don't include this man in your future plans. If and when he is divorced he can always make you an offer. This way you will have an option. Otherwise a year from now you'll be exactly in the same condition. Except for one thing—you'll be one year older!

3. *Spend only your extra time with him*

Treat your time with him the way you would a date. Don't neglect your work, your interests, or your friends to be with him. If he has been in the habit of just dropping by, start breaking the pattern. Tell him you would appreciate a call before he comes over. You certainly wouldn't drop in on him! No need to make it a big issue. He'll get the point.

4. *Begin to look around*

The world is a great big place. Life doesn't begin and end with him. When you limit yourself to one man, it restricts your vision and regulates your emotions. When he's there, you are happy. When he's not there, you wonder what he's doing, where he is, if he's thinking about you, and when he'll be back. This narrow outlook will be obvious to the man. It also makes you a very dull person.

You know there is no truth in the idea of one certain man for one certain woman. You promised "to have and to hold" your former husband "till death do us part." If you are now divorced you know how meaningful *that* was! You don't know who else is out there. If you're longing so strongly for marriage, put yourself in a position to meet eligible men. Your current man is your *least* likely prospect.

5. *Widen your interests*

Relating to one man for several months does put you into a rut. Plus the fact that his marriage limits the places you two can go together. What a tacky way to live. Start doing new things on your own. Sign up for a class at night school. Plan a weekend in the mountains or a day at the beach. Call up some old friends and invite them to dinner. Move around. Look around. Get around.

There is no need to discuss what you are doing when you are not with him. The advice you asked from him can now dwindle down. You can be enthusiastic about what you're learning, but don't mention the other men that will begin to be attracted to you. Let him guess. Most women have a craving to "tell all" to the man of the moment. Try to get over that notion as soon as possible. He may try to keep you back if he feels too threatened. After all, he's got a very good deal.

6. *Stop feeling guilty*

You owe this man absolutely nothing. On the contrary, it is *he* who should be apologizing to you. No woman enjoys the roll of back-street wife. No woman who cares about herself would put up with it. He should not complain about anything constructive you do. I could write an entire book on the way women are controlled by guilt. Husbands make wives feel guilt for their failures. Children hold mothers in slavery by guilt. Friends torture each other with guilt. As far as *this* man is concerned, you should have not one twinge of guilt—now or ever.

The married man who has a sustained relationship outside his marriage based on "love," is a very selfish human being. He will *take* until you are tired of *giving*. That is why you should begin to do these six things immediately! He will either want you more than ever, or he will disappear. Why not bring it to a head. You may be startled at what you'll find out.

A divorcée from the Mid-West wrote to me for advice on the same problem. Her "married friend" loved to come by after work for a candlelight dinner in front of the fireplace. Because her children were small they would have already eaten and gone to bed. This young divorcée didn't work and found her life was slipping into the exact same pattern as when she was married. It was not an unhappy situation. In fact she eagerly looked forward to the nights when *he* would be there.

I suggested she immediately look for work and broaden her horizons. She was young and there was no reason for her to continue this "married life" as an unmarried woman. I also urged her to check on her married friend to see just how "impossible" his marriage was and if divorce was indeed imminent.

It was months before I heard from her again, and when I did hear it was just a brief note to tell me she was getting married—to her "married" friend! She said in her "checking up" she discovered he was not married at all and had two or three other single women like herself who were feeding him, loving him, and waiting for him to get divorced! She said she told him it was all over and he suggested they get married!

I've often wondered how this marriage turned out. Perhaps he was afraid of marriage and this was his way of toying with the idea. Obviously he wanted to be found out and was sufficiently pleased with his arrangement with her to risk marriage. If this man had actually been married, her new independent attitude would have forced him to resolve his situation at home—one way or the other.

I have repeated this phrase ad nauseum, but let me just say it again: *Build your own life.* Don't depend upon men for your happiness. This is the only *true* freedom. You are a desirable, worthwhile, interesting, feeling human being who deserves to be happy. It's the way you were meant to be. Life is always complicated but part of the joy of living is working out your own salvation. So why take on the problems of a discontented married man. He has to solve problems at work. There is no reason he can't resolve his situation at home.

QUESTION TWENTY-EIGHT

I Have Been Remarried About Two Years and I Am Miserable. What Would a Second Divorce Do To Me?

Marriage is a man-made law. Divorce is a man-made remedy. We have laws and remedies to regulate the variables in our society. Marriage and divorce are both legal actions and of themselves do nothing to you, your character or your reputation. However, individual interpretation brings *everything* you do into the world of opinion. Some opinions mean a great deal. Others we don't care a thing in the world about.

Before you jump into a second divorce, make an effort to probe deeply into exactly *why* you are unhappy. This probing and self-discovery will be enormously beneficial to you whether you stay married or pursue a divorce. Begin by listing what could be wrong.

WHAT COULD BE WRONG:

1. Loss of physical interest in each other
2. Personality conflict
3. Financial strain
4. Personal tragedy
5. Different goals
6. Family problems
7. Another woman
8. Another man

WHAT TO DO ABOUT IT:

1. *Loss of physical interest in each other*
   This is certainly not an uncommon complaint. Courtship stimulates a sexual pace that is often never reached again. When the mystery is gone and the chase ended, routine begins. Your lack of interest in each other needs a jolt. You, as the wife, should create situations conducive to lovemaking. If you're honest with yourself you will admit that it isn't hard to excite a man. Give it some thought.
   If your efforts fail, a frank discussion is in order. Find out what's on his mind. You may be turning each other off for very minor reasons. Or they may be major reasons. In either case this situation does not warrant a divorce without some serious questioning. (*See* Question Ten.)
2. *Personality conflict*
   A personality conflict is a severe difference of outlook. If you and your husband differ on religion, politics, choice of friends, mode of leisure, location of home and even time for dinner, you will be unhappy. Conflict does cause pain. No one can survive emotion-

133

ally in such an atmosphere. The only way to treat conflict is to make a pact with each other that you will *only* discuss the matters that need a definitive decision. Religion does not. Where you buy a home does. What happened before your marriage was that each of you in your desire to be pleasing went out of your way to agree with the other. Now you stand pat on your opinions, daring conflict. If you cared enough about each other to get married, you owe it to each other now to *try harder*.

3. *Financial strain*

Nothing puts marriage to a more certain test than a severe change in finances. Tough times either split people apart, or join them tighter than before. Pulling together either makes a strong team or an out-of-step couple. If you are having some bad financial problems, trace them to the cause. If the financial problems are due to natural causes (illness, loss of job, heavy school bills, etc.) then you should pitch in and help.

If the financial strain is due to drinking, gambling, or living over your head, you need help. You certainly do not want to invest your time, labor, and years in a man who has lost control of himself. Reassess your values and your goals. Insist he seek counseling. If he refuses to help himself, save yourself.

There is free budget counseling available through Consumer's Credit Association. You might look them up and solicit help. Professional help in any area of living is valuable, but you must seek it. Help will not come and find you.

4. *Personal tragedy*

If you are genuinely grief-stricken over the death of a loved one, a severe disappointment in your work, or fear for a wayward child, wait awhile before you end your marriage. One pain is not going to cure another. Too many people seek divorce because it seems like an answer, because it occupies their mind, because it is *there*.

A couple married nineteen years were seeking a divorce after the death of a fifteen-year-old son. The mother was so utterly devastated by the tragedy that she would stay in bed for days at a time, cry for hours and hardly touch her food. Her husband was unable to console her. Her grief seemed determined to take over her life.

The husband had to keep going. He had his work and responsibilities. His grief was equally great but he was forced to bear it alone. The wife was too engrossed in her "private" tragedy to reach out to him. Eventually he reached out elsewhere. He began seeing a divorced woman I knew and a familiar pattern developed. The wife, in her selfish grief, had forced additional tragedy into their lives. When divorce became imminent, it wasn't "the other woman" who was to blame at all. The husband simply had no desire to sacrifice his life in useless mourning.

5. *Different goals*

Goals, both short term and long range, are absolutely necessary to a marriage, or any other form of partnership. To progress you must have purpose. You know the individual thrill of personal accomplishment. Do you know the joy of mutual success? Are your dreams becoming fantasies because you don't share them? Do you have any true understanding of what your husband hopes to accomplish in life?

Before you think of divorce again, sit down with your husband and ask him about his hopes, his dreams, his goals. Your husband may be miserable in his job. He could be dreaming of going back to school and becoming a dentist. Or he may hate the city and be secretly dreaming of owning a small ranch.

Tell him your desires also. If you have always wanted to own a needlework shop, work in a bookstore or learn jewelry making—tell him. Once the two of you have shared your long-range goals, plan for them. Decide which goals have priority and keep track of your progress. Working together makes living together a new, more meaningful life.

6. *Family problems*

More harm is done to marriages by "well-meaning" families than can possibly be imagined. The most common complaint is against mothers and mothers-in-law. As ancient as the old jokes are, they were founded in truth. Mothers and mothers-in-law can be big trouble.

If your unhappiness stems from outside influence, get ahold of yourself. Being told by your mother that he's not good enough for you, is no reason to leave him. He may *not* be good enough for you but that is certainly for you to decide. On the other hand his mother may feel she knows all the answers and her ways of doing things are superior to yours. Again, you don't leave your husband to get away from her.

A divorced woman in Chicago wrote me that she had divorced her husband because his mother dominated their life. She would drop in at all hours, lift the lids to see what was cooking, and criticize the wife's housekeeping. The husband refused to stand up to the mother and bitter arguments soon led to divorce. Now, the divorcée wrote, the mother still comes by to see her and tells her how much better she was as a daughter-in-law than the new wife!

Some "well-meaning" relatives do need to be told. Married couples should be free to make their own way. If you are unhappy because of this type of situation, discuss it with your husband. If he refuses to help you, seek some outside help. Talk it over with someone you respect who knows all concerned parties (your doctor, minister, lawyer) A divorce is not necessarily a solution here.

7. *Another woman*

If your husband has told you he's in love with another woman, he could be telling you any number of things. Before you rush out and engage a lawyer, consider what else he could mean.

a. He wants a divorce.

b. He wants you to tell him to straighten up.

c. He wants you to straighten up.

d. He wants you to know he's desirable to other women.

e. He wants to hurt you.

The list is endless but these are some of the best-known reasons.

a. *He wants a divorce.*

How do you handle this first situation? In California if a man wants a divorce—that's it. No fault has to be established, no elaborate games played, no pretense. He simply gives the wife half of all community property (i.e., the property they accumulated together) and walks away. Check into the laws of your state. If you feel, because of his interest in this other woman, that divorce is inevitable, make your demands through your lawyer.

136

Treat him so kindly and politely he'll scratch his head. He'll wonder what's going on. He'll begin to look at you anew. Don't give in to unreasonable demands, but refuse to fight with him. Smile, pour him a drink, and refer him to your lawyer. If he's determined to get a divorce, keep your ladyship.

b. *He wants you to tell him to straighten up.*

Many men (a *great* many men) turn their wives into mothers. In their role of a "bad little boy" the straying husband wants to be found out and spanked. So spank him! Tell him how terrible, just terrible he has been. Tell him he owes you a nice new coat. (Mink, perhaps?) Tell him he has to be home at 6:15 every night and no more business trips without you. He'll feel oh so much better—then he'll go do it all over again.

Divorce is not your only alternative. You can tell him you understand the whole dumb thing, you don't like it, and you don't ever want to hear about it again. You can tell him to go talk to someone who gets paid for listening and giving advice—but to quit boring you. When you don't rise to the occasion, what's the fun? Hopefully this treatment would cure him.

c. *He wants you to straighten up.*

Perhaps your husband is taunting you with another woman to point up something you are doing (or not doing) that is ruining the marriage. Two women I know personally are going through this right now. One is excessively overweight and the husband has done everything from quiet talks with her to publicly calling her "Fats" at a dinner party.

The other wife has become president of her women's club and spends all her time on "club business." When pleas to her to pay attention to him and their children failed, he told her he had found another woman. Both these husbands loved their wives. They don't want to break up their marriages. Both feel the wives owe it to them and to their marriages to try harder.

For a man to want his wife to watch her weight and watch her hours away from home is not being "dominated." You are not going to be less of a woman or less of an individual because you consider the needs of your husband. Think what you

137

could be doing that would cause your husband to find another woman. If there doesn't seem to *be* a cause, he probably does want out of the marriage.

d. *He wants you to know he's desirable to women.*

The husband who taunts, wants you to fly into a jealous rage, fight to get him back, claw to save your nest. Go ahead. Jealousy is a *wild* emotion. Maybe you can throw yourself at his feet, make love on the bathroom floor, or run away together for the weekend.

Again, divorce is not your only alternative. You can say you've known all along how attractive he was (after all, didn't you marry him?) but you have no intention of being a spectator while he runs his own private popularity contest. You can further say you have important things to do in your life and he'd better channel his energies along constructive lines also or the world will pass him by.

e. *He wants to hurt you.*

A husband who tells you about another woman for the sheer evil pleasure of sticking pins in your heart, is sick. He needs some help. Before you take his evilness to your heart and let it poison you, insist he seek some counseling. Don't retaliate by finding men with which to taunt him. That's a dead-end street that leaves you both broken and bitter.

8. *Another man*

If your unhappiness with your present marriage stems from the fact that you've met another man, I still won't recommend divorce as your only alternative. Examine what it is in the new man that you find missing in your husband. Here might be the clue to why you are unhappy. So many times when we feel something is missing in someone else, in reality, what we feel is something missing is ourselves.

I met a very complicated woman in New York who was having an affair with an actor several years her junior. A year prior to this she had had plastic surgery on her nose, something she had always wanted to do. The new nose had made a terrific difference in her looks and she developed an entirely new personality. She considered her new self kittenish and coy, and very much a flirt. Her husband told me she resented the fact that he had married her when she was ugly.

Instead of loving the husband more than ever for

marrying her for her *real* values, she puts him down for being so stupid as to marry an ugly woman. When she looks at her husband she says he reminds her of her crooked nose. I feel that what he reminds her of is her "crooked" personality. A new nose is certainly no reason for a new man.

If you have found a new love interest in your life, consider how he differs from your current husband. You *must* have had some reason to marry him. Has he changed that much? Or is it you? It is quite possible to outgrow any relationship but the growth must be real and lasting. The only accurate test of whether your marriage is over is if you would continue the divorce proceedings were this new man *not* in the offing.

If, after reading all these bases for unhappiness, you feel you would like to seek some counseling before you seek a divorce, do so. There is a great deal of help available. Here are some channels.

● *Your church*

If you have a minister, priest, or rabbi with whom you can talk, do. Don't be afraid, they've heard everything at least once before. If they are able to help you they will. If not, they will refer you to someone who can.

● *Your doctor*

He, too, has heard it all before and is quite able to make recommendations as to what you should do. He can also refer you to a psychiatrist or psychologist he feels best suited to help you.

● *Your lawyer*

Before an attorney presses forward with a divorce he will probe the problems. Because of the number of people he sees with similar problems, he is usually able to tell if a marriage can be saved. He will then recommend help if he feels there is a possibility of reconciliation.

● *The Conciliation Court*

Many states* have a free service called the Concilia-

* The following states have this service: Alaska, Arizona, California, Hawaii, Illinois, Indiana, Michigan, Missouri, Montana, Nebraska, North Dakota, Oregon, Utah, Wisconsin.

tion Court. Here, either the husband or wife may go for free counseling. A trained social worker will listen to the problems and try to help. If he or she feels the marriage can be saved, both partners will be asked to participate in the counseling.

Often a judge will set aside a divorce proceeding and refer a couple to counseling. But again, you don't have to be involved in a divorce proceeding to use the services of the Conciliation Court. They are anxious to help as many people as possible. If you feel you would like to talk to a professional counselor and live in a state where this service is available, look up the Court in the phone book—under state or county offices. Then call and make an appointment. You need no one's consent or permission to do this.

The least likely place to get sound, impartial advice is from your family and friends. Don't poll people. If you sincerely want help go where real help is available. There is no law that says you should be unhappy. That is why we *do* have divorce. Don't be miserable. If you have sought help, made an effort, but still feel your marriage is over, end it legally.

I don't lightly recommend divorce. However, I am far more interested in saving women than in saving marriages. That applies to myself also. I was married for the second time about six hours when I knew it was wrong. In six weeks I knew it was impossible. In six months it was over. I had written *The Divorcée's Handbook* the previous year and I thought I knew all the answers. What was going to happen now? I could just hear the laughter, "Author of *The Divorcée's Handbook* divorced again!" I felt I was destined to be the joke of the year. All the concern about "them" out there. All the worry about what "they" would say. All the wasted hours thinking up "logical" excuses. But do you know what actually happened? When I finally raised my head and looked around, nobody was even watching.

Each person in this world is so concerned about his own problems that he has precious little time to waste on yours. Of course there are reactions that are painful. My family was embarrassed and my children confused. Plus it was painful to admit to new people I met (especially eligible men) that I was a double divorcée. But the chance to start over again was a glorious feeling that overshadowed all else. I have since remarried and I am enormously happy. Because you *make* a mistake in life, doesn't mean you *are* a mistake.

A dear friend of mine is about to be married for the fourth time. Not yet thirty-six, "public opinion" has been quite hard on her. But I know, and her family knows, and her true friends know, that she is in love with her husband-to-be in a new, more mature, more giving, more complete way than ever before. Because she has now found herself and likes herself, this man is seeing new qualities in her. If I were a gambler I would bet heavily on this marriage.

Many multi-married people are multi-married for very obvious reasons. Until an individual takes the time and invests the effort in honestly coming to grips with himself, the same mistakes will be repeated. One of the most glaring mistakes of the multi-married is the incredibly poor judgment they show in choice of mates. A poor marriage risk will *always* be a poor marriage risk.

If you do pursue a second divorce make a solemn pact with yourself *not* to jump into another relationship until you have spent time working with yourself, on yourself. You cannot possibly begin to reach your potential in any area until you have engaged in a critical self-examination. Remove the mental barriers you have erected to obscure your view of you. It isn't always "his fault" or "their error" or "her stupidity." You are only in competition with your opinion of who you are and what you can do. So lift your sights. Elevate your goals. Think big. Demand to be successful. Accept nothing less than honest values. Live happiness!

P.S. If you have further questions, write to me. I will be delighted to share my ideas with you.

LOUISE MONTAGUE ATHEARN
P.O Box 651
San Mateo California 94401

A Man's (and Lawyer's) Point of View

The author of this book is my wife. In 1967—long before she met me—she wrote *The Divorcée's Handbook* which proved to be an enormously successful book. I read the book and after dating her several times, her commonsense made me decide she was the girl for me.

As a lawyer with considerable divorce experience as well as experience in handling estates for widows, it was the suggestion of the publishers of this book that I write a concluding chapter. My viewpoint is that of a man *and* a lawyer who's job it has been to advise thousands of formerly married women.

When a woman comes to me for a divorce I invariably remind her that she must expect to feel a certain emotional trauma. Nothing her lawyer or anyone else can say is going to spare her this emotional wrench. Prepared for the trauma, she will find it easier to live through the ordeal. Her consolation is that millions of women have gone through this emotional hell before her and come out happier and frequently better for it.

The first and most obvious situation a widowed or divorced woman faces is filling in certain physical voids in her life. She is fortunate if she already has a job. If she doesn't, she should get one. Fixing up her house and making it a more pleasant place to live or fixing it up because she has to sell it and move into a smaller house or apartment is a challenge to her creative instincts as an interior designer, a landscape architect, a businesswoman. In addition, it takes physical effort which in itself is therapeutic—minor carpentry, plumbing, painting, and wall papering. I know of one woman who, after her divorce, bought an older house, refurbished it to a large extent with her own hands, added a basement apartment which she could rent to college students. The rent enabled her to make the home loan payments. At the same time her children, who were twelve and fourteen, learned to perform household chores which enabled her to go to school to get a degree in clinical psychology. She became an enormous success as a mother, as a homemaker, and in her profession.

The secret of her success is that she organized herself, her life, and went to work.

The second problem situation frequently facing the formerly married woman is raising children alone. Often the working mother is the better mother because, while she takes time to help the children organize their school work and social activities, she doesn't have time to dote upon or smother them. Encouraging them to have weekend and summer jobs to help with finances is one of the best things any mother can do for her children.

Rearing children in these times is not easy. Rearing them without a live-in father can further complicate the job. Here are factors to be aware of:

1. The standards and verities by which our parents and grandparents were raised have to a large extent been swept away.

2. The affluence of our society has created various teenage sub-cultures to whose standards and attitudes youths assiduously, often slavishly, conform. Often this is a bafflement to parents and other adults.

3. The acceleration of change in our times has been so great that new problems and new situations arise and often just as quickly disappear before we even have a solution for them.

4. The so-called new freedoms and affluence now permit teen-agers to travel, live in communes and with one another in ways unheard of by a generation raised just ten or fifteen years ago.

It is important to remember that not all of this is bad. By and large young people have an easier, less inhibited, mentally healthier, and far more realistic attitude toward the opposite sex than we or previous generations had. I am not suggesting that the younger generation is promiscuous. I think I would rather have my nineteen-year-old daughter live with a young man and know what he is like and what living with a man is like than to have her marry at nineteen and spend the next five, ten, or twenty years regretting the marriage.

Because you and your children are individual and unique, there are two things you must do: One, let your children know that you love them. Whatever problems they have, let them know they can bring them to you and discuss them freely. Two, the lines of communication between parent and child must be kept open. Sometimes these lines will be temporarily cut, but you can and must repair them. Psychologists and family counselors confirm this.

The third great category of problems and questions facing the single woman is finances. Managing money is an art. You can learn it if you make up your mind to learn it. Start by making a budget that you can live with and stay within that budget. Don't try to keep up with the Joneses. Who are the Joneses anyhow?

You can find many ways to save money. Close your charge accounts. Pay cash. I think the banks and department stores are the biggest culprits in the country—Public Enemy Number One—for encouraging the use of charge accounts, charge plates, and credit cards. These are fine for a businessman on an expense account, but not for you. The interest you pay over the years could send your children to college, buy a piece of investment property, buy a home, or finance a trip to Europe. In this area remember you are not an expert but you can become one.

Consult your banker about ways to save your money. If you are a widow who has inherited a tidy little chunk, consult a professional investment counselor. Consult an accountant on ways to set up your home books and save your money. Don't buy stocks that promise to make you rich next month. The speculative stock is for the very sophisticated.

Buy a used automobile, a used washing machine, a used TV set or used furniture rather than go into debt buying these items new. I have seen the heartache and misery caused by women who bought on credit. I have seen women lose their homes, their automobiles, and their furniture because they bought on credit. You can learn to make money a leverage in your favor, rather than a leverage against you.

The final category of problems facing the formerly married woman is her association with men. Most women would rather be married than be single (and I say this as a supporter of Women's Liberation before there was a Movement). There is nothing to be ashamed of about this desire. When you're widowed or divorced, it's natural to want to remarry. The widow should not feel that by remarrying she is being disloyal to her late husband. Psychologists tell us that when a spouse remarries after the death of a loved one, this is really a great tribute to the departed. It indicates the marriage was good and that the living spouse wants to find similar happiness in another marriage.

The divorced woman has a little different viewpoint. Hers was an unhappy marriage, and for this reason she may fear to remarry. Again, it's wrong to make blanket statements about marriage. Each union is as unique as the individual partners.

Now let me offer some thoughts from the man's point of view on how a woman should go about finding that man who is right for her. I was a bachelor until forty-one and therefore acquired some insight from a personal as well as a professional point of view.

First, don't idealize men *or* marriage. Such idealization is unrealistic and belongs only in mediocre movies and bad novels. Films and novels are rarely models for life. The ideal you seek in a man is only ideal. A man has his problems just as a woman has her problems. They may be different but they are just as real. His problems can run the whole gamut—business problems, financial problems, career problems, job problems, problems with his ex-wife, problems with his children, hangups about sex (yes, men have just as many hang-ups about sex and I think in some ways more hang-ups than women). He may have personal insecurities about himself. We all have certain insecurities. Finding and marrying a man is never a solution to your personal problems. It is exchanging one set of problems for a new set.

Second, spend time analyzing the men you meet. Not many women look below the surface. I know an exotically beautiful, charming, and brilliant young woman who could have had any man in town. Instead she chose a man who "slapped her around." She mistook his conduct for masculine strength. After the marriage she discovered that this was masculine weakness; only a strong man can be gentle.

For a woman to attempt to analyze a man and for a man to attempt the same of a woman is to undertake a task that has fascinated and confounded the human species since the beginning of mankind. Certainly the first person to come up with an easy, sure-fire formula will have his fortune made many times over. Yet the enormity of the task should never prevent us from trying.

Begin with yourself. Analyze what it is that attracts you to a particular man. This involves a certain amount of self-analysis. It may be that you are drawn to him because of your own feelings of inadequacy. If he is weak, a drifter, unable to hold a job, frequently in scrapes with the law and poorly adjusted to society in general, there is probably something wrong with you if you are attracted to him. Is it that you want to be his mother and protect him from the world? Is it that you like to feel the power of being the dominant person, the boss in the relationship? The castrating female married to the man who likes to be castrated is not an unusual phenomenon. It is a sick relationship that does not bode well for the future.

Take the case of the woman who likes to be slapped around—physically or emotionally. The female masochist married to the male sadist is not an unusual relationship. Again it's not a relationship that leads to happiness.

Examples of emotionally sick relationships are multitudinous. Many marriages are built upon just such a meshing of neuroses. Few of these marriages can be described as good, sound, or lasting. Work to conquer your own neurosis. Don't perpetuate it in a relationship with a male counterpart.

Analyze the physical attraction. There is, or should be, a certain undefinable chemistry between you and the man to whom you are attracted. This chemistry is essential to a marriage. I have known many marriages to stumble along because there existed a good sexual relationship when every other reason for the marriage had disappeared. At the same time I have known marriages that had a lot to recommend them fail because there was not a satisfactory sex relationship. The chemistry of a relationship is frequently mistaken for love. The chemistry is essential, but it is only one part. It is not all there is to love. You need it, but you need more.

Another facet to analyze is his attitude toward sex. If a man is constantly seeking new conquests, the chances are very good that he is subconsciously worried about his masculinity. The need to have new and frequent conquests suggests he is trying to prove something to himself. This man is a bad marriage risk. Of course you want a man who enjoys sex, but why be one of many? The real test of a man's powers is if he is able to bring you to your full enjoyment potential.

Another consideration is what a man has accomplished as a man. Does he have a good job and apply himself? Has his business or career grown? Is he ambitious? What are these ambitions? Do they coincide with yours? Is his career, business, or job one that you could be happy to have him continue? If you can't accept his occupation, ambitions, and goals, he is not for you. The probability is that you are not going to remake him, so don't try.

Consider a man's temperament and character. Is he patient, kind, gentle, tolerant? Does he have a sense of humor? Possession of these characteristics indicates emotional stability and the ability to get along with people, including you. There is a give and take in all relationships, especially marriage. His ability to get along with others is a good indication of his ability to get along in a marriage.

On the other hand, if he throws tantrums, sulks, has fixations or is unduly suspicious, he probably has some serious neurotic difficulties which would not make him easy to live with. Beware of the man who is unduly jealous of you, your friends, your job or career, or the other men in your life. At first this may seem flattering. It is really a sign that he is unsure of himself and he is therefore unable to trust people—including you.

Look at a man's friends. What are they like and how long has he had them? If you can't stand his friends, you probably won't like him too well after marriage either. If he has responsible friends of long standing, this is a good indication of his career.

Is this man a giver or a taker? There are a lot of men who will take everything they can—your affection, your love, your time, your energy, your food, your liquor, the use of your apartment, the use of your bed. Sharing the bed with him may be pleasant, but freeloaders are not interested in you. Their own pleasures come first. Extricate yourself as soon as possible. The taker is incapable of the profound relationship which marriage represents. The man who gives as much or more than he takes indicates that he understands that a healthy relationship must be one of give and take.

Background is of vital importance and too often overlooked. At first blush the premise of this question may seem archaic. Certainly it is possible for two people of widely differing cultures, religions and backgrounds to bridge these chasms, but it is by no means easy. A deeply religious person raised by the standards and tenets of her faith might find it difficult and perhaps impossible to live with a militant atheist. A modern American, liberated young woman would find it very difficult being married to a man raised in the Middle East, whose religion permits four wives and whose culture requires the wives to be servile.

Experience shows that people with similar backgrounds, similar goals, similar ambitions, aspirations, cultures, education, and religion have a better chance of making a happy marriage. Doubtless you may recall many examples of happy and successful marriages where the backgrounds were extremely divergent. Nevertheless I have seen too many cases where wide divergencies led to short marriages.

Another important attribute a man must have is sufficient self-esteem. Don't confuse "ego trip" with self-esteem. Displays of ego are usually a cover-up for feelings of inadequacy or inferiority. Honest self-assurance and self-esteem are the opposite. A person with true self-esteem does not indulge in antics to feed his ego. He is not all wrapped up in his own ego and his own problems. He has sufficient assurance to give love and to accept yours. When two people have attained this degree of maturity they are capable of a great love.

After having analyzed the man or men in your life, consider the relationship from the man's point of view. Face the fact that there are more women than men. Therefore men have a wider range of choice, not only in numbers but in age brackets. It is not uncommon for a man of forty-five to marry a woman twenty-five.

To meet the competition, consider what a man seeks in a woman. There are obvious things that he doesn't want. He doesn't want a lush. If he does, he probably has a drinking problem, too.

Physical attractiveness is an undeniable asset no matter what your sex. It is not difficult for observant and intelligent persons to make themselves physically attractive, regardless of natural endowments. If you watch your weight, take care of your complexion and hair, dress neatly and exude a pleasant fragrance you have covered most of the bases.

When it comes to makeup, men usually are more turned on by naturalness then by artificiality.

Now comes the question of availability. Be available, but not a doormat or pusher. If you like him let him know that you enjoy his company. Be willing to accept spur-of-the-moment dates. But don't be the person who is hanging around all the time when he is otherwise occupied or who is constantly calling him at his job.

Sex? Yes, of course. The question is always when and under what circumstances. Don't be afraid to say yes when the time is right. Jumping into bed with him the first night is not a great idea. He will like it, but he will probably think you do that the first night with every other man you date. Men are not always charitable in their judgments the next day. There are unpleasant words for the woman who says "yes" too readily.

Don't be afraid to say no. It's hard to respect the easy lay and a man *does* want to respect the woman he gets serious about. This talk of respect may sound old-fashioned. It's not. It's telling it as it is, because in the minds of most of us the sex act represents an intimacy and affection between a man

148

and a woman. The person who appears insensitive to this somehow loses the respect of the other.

Let's talk about age. Veneration of youth in American culture is an unfortunate sign of our cultural immaturity; it certainly prevents our culture from using the wisdom and the talents of the old.

But momentarily we are stuck with the cult of youth. Don't let your age become an obsession with you. If you are forty don't try to dress and act like a twenty-year-old. That turns anyone off fast. Anyone can be youthful in appearance and attitude and at the same time be mature. As for sex, there's nothing like experience. A mature man really wants a woman who appreciates and understands him, which is hard for a very young woman to do, while a woman near his own age can.

As a final suggestion, please consider this. Many people want to get married because it's a good deal for them. Such people look upon marriage as a solution to their problems—financial, social, and psychological. The mates they choose are almost incidental. Consciously or unconsciously a woman or man knows this and resents it. Obviously this approach to marriage does not bode well for future happiness and is one that should be avoided.

We attract a partner primarily because we let her or him know that we are interested in him or her, his or her problems, his or her job, his or her business, his or her world. You should also let a man or woman you are interested in know that you can help that person. Let him know that he is going to be much better off with you than without you. When you convince him of this you have him for good. When my wife and I were courting she told me, "Athearn, I'll be the best thing that ever happened to you." In my heart I know she was right and now she has me forever.

Don't be the flighty person who is constantly bringing a lover problems. Some people even create problems just to maintain a high pitch of excitement, drama, and discord. The hypochondriac is but one example.

From my personal and professional experience I could give you many examples of the neurotic person who spells trouble. But an interesting job, community involvement, and responsibility keep things in proper perspective. Most men want a woman who takes time to understand them and has concern for their wants. If you are totally involved in "self," men will feel you have little time for them.

If you are the organized, self-reliant woman we have been

149

talking about you're not going to be neurotic. You are doing your own thing, you're standing on your own feet. This makes you immensely attractive to men. This is *the* way to get a man. It doesn't involve seduction or tricks of makeup. You will attract men because you are an interesting person. You are interesting because you are *interested* not only in him but in all things. You are interesting because you are vital, you enjoy life, and you are living. Men will seek you out in droves. That is the message of this book. My many years as a lawyer and a bachelor confirm this, over and over again.

FORDEN ATHEARN

San Mateo, California